D1480400

Christa Wolf

Twayne's World Authors Series

German Literature

David O'Connell, Editor
Georgia State University

TWAS 877

CHRISTA WOLF
Courtesy of the German Information Center

Christa Wolf

Gail Finney

University of California, Davis

Twayne Publishers
New York

Twayne's World Authors Series No. 877

Christa Wolf
Gail Finney

Twayne Publishers
1633 Broadway
New York, NY 10019

Library of Congress Cataloging-in-Publication Data

Finney, Gail.
    Christa Wolf / Gail Finney.
        p.   cm. — (Twayne's world authors series ; no. 877. German literature)
    Includes bibliographical references and index.
    ISBN 0-8057-4622-6 (alk. paper)
    1. Wolf, Christa. 2. Authors, German—20th century—Biography.
I. Title. II. Series.   III. Series: Twayne's world authors series ;
TWAS 878. IV. Series: Twayne's world authors series.   German literature.
PT2685.O36Z674   1999
833'.914—dc21   98-33257
                                              CIP

Contents

Preface

Christa Wolf is acknowledged to be the best-known German woman writer of the twentieth century. She played a significant role in East German cultural politics, has been awarded numerous prizes and honors in both East and West Germany, has given readings and speeches all over the world, has been hosted and celebrated far and wide, and has seen her books translated into more than a dozen languages. She did more than any other writer from the former German Democratic Republic to place the literature of that country on a global stage.

Yet while Wolf's life and career are distinguished, they are also representative, in terms of both historical and aesthetic trends, of the lives and careers of other writers of her generation. Perhaps most notably, by virtue of her birth in 1929, Wolf belongs to the generation of Germans typically characterized as "blessed by being born too late"—too late, that is, to have been complicit in the crimes of the Third Reich. Although her childhood coincided with Hitler's dictatorship, a fact with which much of her work attempts to come to terms, like her contemporaries she was young and ideologically unbiased enough in 1945 to take an active role in shaping the new socialist Germany that rose from the ashes of the Second World War. Similarly, like many of her literary colleagues, she began writing with a deep commitment to the new socialist state and followed the tenets of socialist realism, then subsequently broke with this political and aesthetic program. Yet she branched off in experimental directions of her own, so that a good deal of her work emerges as extreme or even unique in GDR fiction. And, although like many of her fellow writers in the German Democratic Republic she eventually became highly critical of the regime, her criticism has been founded throughout on a doctrine that can best be described as utopian humanism. Finally, while most of her work is autobiographical, it simultaneously strives to be representative of larger concerns, such as the development of her country, women's issues, or world peace. Wolf's confrontations with material from her life are intended to yield results productive for the society in which she lives. This volume, a critical study of Wolf's life and work, presents her career in its combination of typicality and distinctiveness.

Acknowledgments

I would like to thank Olin Library of Cornell University for providing me with a faculty study during my residence in Ithaca in the summer of 1997. Use of the study greatly facilitated my work on this book.

I owe a major debt of gratitude to Harvey Himelfarb, former vice provost for academic planning and personnel at the University of California, Davis. Without his understanding and flexibility in adjusting my work schedule as his faculty assistant in the fall of 1997, I could not have completed this volume in a timely manner.

My sincere appreciation goes to Peter Rock and Caroline Schaumann for their thoughtful and genuinely beneficial comments on chapters of the manuscript.

Permission to reprint the following essays, in part or in toto, with editorial revisions, is gratefully acknowledged: "Crossing the Gender Wall: Narrative Strategies in GDR Fictions of Sexual Metamorphosis," in *Neverending Stories: Toward a Critical Narratology,* ed. Ann Fehn, Ingeborg Hoesterey, and Maria Tatar (Princeton: Princeton University Press, 1992), 163–78, and "The Christa Wolf Controversy: Wolf's *Sommerstück* as Chekhovian Commentary," *Germanic Review* 67 (Summer 1992): 106–11, published by Heldref Publications. The latter article is reprinted with permission of the Helen Dwight Reid Educational Foundation.

Chronology

1929   Born on 18 March in Landsberg an der Warthe (today Polish Gorzów Wielkopolski). Father, Otto Ihlenfeld, runs a grocery store.

1939–1945   Attends school in Landsberg.

1945   Flees with family to Mecklenburg.

1945–1946   Clerical assistant to mayor of Gammelin, near Schwerin.

1946   Attends high school in Schwerin. Is admitted briefly to a sanatorium for lung ailments.

1947   Moves to Bad Frankenhausen (Kyffhäuser).

1949   Completes high school examinations (Abitur) in Bad Frankenhausen. Joins SED (Socialist Unity Party).

1949–1953   Studies German literature at the universities in Jena and Leipzig. *Diplomarbeit* (thesis) under Hans Mayer on "Problems of Realism in the Work of Hans Fallada."

1951   Marries Gerhard Wolf, Germanist and essayist, born 1928.

1952   Birth of daughter Annette.

1953–1959   Research assistant for German Writers' Union (until 1955). On staff of *Neue deutsche Literatur* (from 1954). Chief editor for Neues Leben (press specializing in publications for young people), 1956.

1955   First of numerous trips to Soviet Union.

1955–1976   Member of executive committee of Writers' Union, GDR.

1956   Birth of daughter Katrin.

1958–1959   Editor of *Neue deutsche Literatur.*

1959–1962   Moves to Halle. Works in railroad car factory under influence of Bitterfeld Movement. Becomes involved in "Circles of Writing Workers." Works as freelance editor for Mitteldeutscher Verlag. Edits several anthologies of contemporary East German literature. Allegedly supplies information to the Stasi (Secret Police).

1960   First of many trips to the Federal Republic of Germany.

1961   Publication of *Moskauer Novelle*. Receives Artists' Prize of the City of Halle.

Since 1962   Lives as freelance author in or near Berlin.

1963   Publication of *Der geteilte Himmel* (trans. *Divided Heaven,* 1965). Receives Heinrich Mann Prize of the Academy of Arts of the GDR.

1963–1967   Candidate of the Central Committee of the SED.

1964   DEFA film of *Der geteilte Himmel* (director Konrad Wolf). Receives National Prize Third Class of the Academy of Arts of the GDR. Gives speech at the Second Bitterfeld Conference. Visits the Auschwitz trials in Frankfurt/Main.

1965   Becomes member of Pen Center, GDR. Participates in 11th Plenum of SED and in International PEN Convention in Yugoslavia. Reading tour in Finland.

1968   Publication of *Nachdenken über Christa T.* (trans. *The Quest for Christa T.,* 1970).

1969   Reading tour in Sweden.

1972   Publication of *Lesen und Schreiben: Aufsätze und Prosastücke* (trans. *The Reader and the Writer: Essays, Sketches, Memories,* 1977). Publication of *Till Eulenspiegel* (together with Gerhard Wolf). Refuses Wilhelm Raabe Prize of the City of Braunschweig. Sojourn in Paris. Travels to Poland. Receives Theodor Fontane Prize for Art and Literature.

1974   Publication of *Unter den Linden: Drei unwahrscheinliche Geschichten* (trans. in *What Remains and Other Stories,* 1993). Becomes member of Academy of Arts of the GDR. Max Kade German Writer-in-Residence, Oberlin College, Oberlin, Ohio.

1975   DEFA film *Till Eulenspiegel* (director Rainer Simon); reading tour in Switzerland.

1976   Publication of *Kindheitsmuster* (trans. *A Model Childhood/Patterns of Childhood,* 1980). Signs "Open Letter" protesting Wolf Biermann's expatriation. Is dismissed from the executive committee of the Berlin chapter of the Writers' Union of the GDR.

1977   Receives Literature Prize of the City of Bremen.

1978   Conducts guest lectures at University of Edinburgh, Scotland. Participates in International PEN Convention in Stockholm.

1979   Publication of *Kein Ort. Nirgends* (trans. *No Place on Earth,* 1982). Publication of *Fortgesetzter Versuch: Aufsätze, Gespräche, Essays.* Becomes member of German Academy for Language and Literature, Darmstadt.

1980   Publication of *Gesammelte Erzählungen* (trans. in *What Remains and Other Stories,* 1993). Receives Georg Büchner Prize of the German Academy for Language and Literature. Travels to Greece.

1981   Becomes member of the Academy of Arts, West Berlin. Participates in the "Berlin Meeting for the Promotion of Peace."

1982   Guest lectureship in poetics, University of Frankfurt/Main. Theatrical premiere of *Till Eulenspiegel,* Hannover. Radio version of *Kein Ort. Nirgends,* read by Gerhard Wolf in WDR. Reading tour in France.

1983   Publication of *Kassandra* and of *Voraussetzungen einer Erzählung: Kassandra. Frankfurter Poetik-Vorlesungen* (trans. *Cassandra: A Novel and Four Essays,* 1984). Receives Schiller Prize. Guest professorship at Ohio State University; receives honorary doctorate there. Gives readings in New York, Los Angeles, San Francisco. Reading tour in West Germany.

1984   Becomes member of the European Academy of Arts and Sciences, Paris. Receives Franz Nabl Prize of the City of Graz. Reading tours in Austria and Italy.

1985   Publication of *"Ins Ungebundene gehet eine Sehnsucht." Gesprächsraum Romantik: Prosa. Essays* (with Gerhard Wolf). Is named Honorary Fellow of the Modern Language Association. Receives Austrian National Prize for European Literature. Receives honorary doctorate, University of Hamburg. Reading tour in France.

1986   Becomes member of the Free Academy of the Arts, Hamburg. Participates in PEN Convention in Hamburg. Travels to Greece and Spain.

1987   Publication of *Die Dimension des Autors: Essays und Aufsätze, Reden und Gespräche 1959–1985* (selections trans. in *The Fourth Dimension: Interviews with Christa Wolf,* 1988 and *The Author's Dimension: Selected* Essays, 1993). Publication of *Störfall: Nachrichten eines Tages* (trans. *Accident: A Day's News,* 1989). Receives National Prize First Class of the GDR for Art and Literature. Guest professorship at the Technical University of Zurich. Receives Geschwister Scholl Prize of the City of Munich.

1988   Publication of *Ansprachen.*

1989   Publication of *Sommerstück.* Withdraws from the SED in June. Publishes many articles, holds discussions, and gives speeches, including speech on 4 November at Alexanderplatz.

1990   Publication of *Im Dialog: Aktuelle Texte* and of *Was bleibt* (trans. in *What Remains and Other Stories,* 1993). Film version of "Selbstversuch" (trans. "Self-Experiment," in *What Remains and Other Stories*) for GDR television (director Peter Vogel). Receives Premio Mondello in Palermo for Italian edition of *Sommerstück.* Receives honorary doctorates from University of Hildesheim and Free University of Brussels. Receives Officier de l'Ordre des Arts et des Lettres, Paris.

1991   Becomes honorary member of the American Academy and Institute of Arts and Letters.

1992–1993 Visiting scholar at Getty Center for the History of Art and Humanities in Santa Monica, California.

1993   Withdraws in March from the Academies of Arts of Berlin, East and West.

1994   Publication of *Auf dem Weg nach Tabou: Texte 1990–1994* (trans. *Parting from Phantoms: Selected Writings, 1990–1994,* 1997). Receives Rahel Varnhagen von Ense Medal of the City of Berlin. Is admitted to Academy of Arts, Berlin/Brandenburg.

1996   Publication of *Medea: Stimmen* (trans. *Medea: A Modern Retelling,* 1998).

Chapter One
Wolf's Life

Christa Wolf was born on 18 March 1929 in Landsberg an der Warthe (today the town of Gorzów Wielkopolski in Poland); she was followed a few years later by a younger brother. Her father, Otto Ihlenfeld, owned a grocery business in which he was assisted by his wife. As members of the petite bourgeoisie, the Ihlenfelds conformed to the system where conformity was required; although Hitler came to power four years after Christa was born, her family cannot be said to have been fanatical Nazis.[1] Christa was enthusiastic about soldiers and war, however, and as was expected of girls of her generation, she served the Führer as a member of the League of German Girls (*Bund Deutscher Mädchen,* or *BDM*). As we learn from her autobiographical novel *Kindheitsmuster* (1976; *Patterns of Childhood*), the young Christa's feelings of loyalty toward the Führer were strong; the following observation from the novel has much to say not only about her motivations but about Hitler's enormous success with the German people: "Sometime or other [in her first three years] [the reasonable child] learned that being obedient and being loved are one and the same thing."[2]

During the war years, from 1939 to 1945, Christa Ihlenfeld attended high school in Landsberg. Her youth effectively came to an end in 1945 when her family was forced to flee the approaching Red Army while her father was still in a Russian prisoner-of-war camp. Christa had already begun to gather impressions of the dark sides of war from her mother, whose view of things tended toward the negative. But in the course of the family's flight from Landsberg, Christa was directly exposed to some of the horrors of war, and of this war in particular, as she witnessed emaciated women in concentration camp uniforms relieving themselves in public by the side of the road, along with other graphic manifestations of misery and death. Not surprisingly, Christa Ihlenfeld burned her diary after the war was over, an act echoed by the protagonists of several of the author's literary works—by Vera Brauer in *Moskauer Novelle* (1961), Rita Seidel in *Der geteilte Himmel* (1963; *Divided Heaven*), the title character of *Nachdenken über Christa T* (1968; *The Quest for Christa T.),* and Nelly Jordan in *Kindheitsmuster.*

From the end of the war until 1946, Christa Ihlenfeld worked as a clerical assistant to the mayor in Gammelin, near the Mecklenburg town of Schwerin. In Schwerin she also continued high school and spent some time in a sanatorium for lung ailments. In 1947 the family moved to Bad Frankenhausen on the Kyffhäuser, where Christa took her *Abitur,* or examinations at the end of high school, at the age of 20 in 1949. That same year, which saw the founding of the two new German states, the Federal Republic of Germany in the West and the German Democratic Republic in the East, she joined the SED, or Socialist Unity Party of East Germany. It might appear that the transition from fascism to socialism was a relatively smooth one for Christa Ihlenfeld, insofar as both are one-party, totalitarian systems that depend on the subordination of the individual to the state or community at large. But it is important to keep in mind the role that her reading of Marx and Engels played in her growing belief in the new East German state and its party, which at the time of her entrance into the SED was very strong.

From 1949 to 1953 Christa studied German literature at the universities in Jena and Leipzig. In 1951 she married a fellow student, Gerhard Wolf, born in 1928 in Bad Frankenhausen. From that point on the two worked together on film projects and anthologies of contemporary German literature. In addition, Gerhard Wolf wrote essays on such subjects as GDR poetry and books on Louis Fürnberg, Johannes Bobrowski, and Hölderlin and along the way garnered numerous prizes.[3] The Wolfs had two daughters: Annette, born in 1952, and Katrin, who followed in 1956.

One of Christa Wolf's most influential professors was Dr. Hans Mayer, the controversial Germanist who moved in 1948 from Frankfurt/ Main to Leipzig in his search for a humane socialism in the new eastern sector of Germany. During the 1950s he became a leading intellectual figure whom many students of German literature sought to hear lecture at some point during their studies. That his hopes for East Germany were not fulfilled was evident by 1963, when he failed to return to the GDR following a trip to the Wagner Festival in Bayreuth. During his tenure in the East, he served as the advisor for Christa Wolf's 1953 thesis entitled "Problems of Realism in the Work of Hans Fallada."

In 1953 Christa Wolf began working as a research assistant for the German Writers' Union, and she soon became a literary critic for its periodical *Neue deutsche Literatur,* for which she served as editor from 1958 to 1959. In 1955 she became a member of the executive committee of the Writers' Union, a position she retained through 1976, and in 1956 she became the chief editor of the publishing house Neues Leben, which spe-

cialized in books for young people. During these years Wolf, with her res-
olutely antifascist convictions, came to be regarded as a leading representative of the East German literary world; concomitantly, her career began
to acquire a privileged status that it has never lost. She made the first of
several trips to the Soviet Union in 1955; the first of numerous visits to
the Federal Republic of Germany followed in 1960.

In 1959 Wolf's young family moved to Halle on the Saale. Already
then the city stank of the industrial pollution that, on the opening of the
Berlin Wall 30 years later, would be revealed as prevalent virtually
everywhere in the GDR. Working in Halle as a freelance editor for the
Mitteldeutscher Verlag, Wolf published several anthologies of contemporary German literature. But she soon became engaged in a very different kind of activity that would prove to be at least as significant for her
own work. At a memorable conference involving the authors of the Mitteldeutscher Verlag that was held in 1959 in the Bitterfeld Electrochem-
ical Conglomerate, party head Walter Ulbricht exhorted workers to
"storm the heights of culture" and urged writers to "get into the facto-
ries." Inspired by the latter charge, Wolf spent some time working in a
railroad car factory. The "Bitterfeld Way," which enjoyed a certain cur-
rency in the first half of the 1960s and encouraged a breakdown of the
barrier between worker and intellectual in the hope that a new kind of
socialist citizen would evolve, left its mark on several works of GDR literature, including Wolf's *Der geteilte Himmel.* The Wolfs' sojourn in
Halle was more short-lived than Christa Wolf's experiment with the
Bitterfeld Way. In 1962 the family moved to the cultural center of East
Germany, Berlin, living first near the Wall in Kleinmachnow and later
in the Fontanestrasse in the vicinity of the Friedrichstrasse, moving from
there to Kleinmachnow only during the summer months.

Upon moving to Berlin, Wolf established herself as a freelance
author. At the same time she became increasingly involved in politics
and cultural politics during the 1960s. She was a candidate for the Central Committee of the SED from 1963 to 1967. In 1964 she received the
National Prize Third Class of the Academy of Arts of the GDR, and the
same year she made a speech at the Second Bitterfeld Conference. She
became a member of the Pen Center, GDR, in 1965. By 1967 her name
had vanished from the list of party candidates, and by 1968 she had
been reprimanded by both the SED and the Writers' Union. Her position vis-à-vis her country was gradually shifting from spokeswoman to
judge. If she had always been critical in her writings, she was becoming,
with *Nachdenken über Christa T.,* quasi-confrontational.

The "Fragment eines Frauenporträts" (Fragment of a woman's portrait), published in 1972 by Wolf's fellow East German writer Günter de Bruyn, succeeds in evoking the complexities of Wolf's character by describing her facial expressions:

> This face is not allowed to laugh, he thinks, although he has seen it laughing, and far from rarely. Smiling would be alright, but not good. What is totally and absolutely unimaginable is cynicism. [This face] would sooner look mean. There are people who know it like that, who don't forget it and who would paint it like that. That would also be possible, but that would offer nothing of her essence, nothing at all. Warmth? Melancholy? Benevolence?
>
> He tries to bring the face to a position of repose, to let it relax, to keep it free of emotion, in order to let out only that which is in it, by nature, in the face itself. And he immediately has it: reflectiveness. Of course, what could have been more obvious? After all, the woman has her own style. But what reflectiveness is without melancholy? And without uneasiness?[4]

A brief survey of Wolf's work will set the stage for a more detailed treatment, in subsequent chapters, of the major phases in her evolution as a writer. Because she has worked above all in the prose genres of novel, short narrative, and short story, this study will pay special attention to the development of her narrative style. With its particular melding of subjective voice; autobiographical elements; and documentary material from history, the media, and science, Wolf's fiction reflects her constant search for narrative truth as well as her often-cited recognition of the "difficulty of saying 'I,' " a phrase that points to her fascination with individual identity and its genesis.

The earliest stage of Wolf's fictional productivity, yielding the narratives *Moskauer Novelle* and *Der geteilte Himmel* coincides with her adherence to the doctrine of socialist realism. *Moskauer Novelle* is in fact so doctrinaire that Wolf herself later compared it to a political tract.[5] Both works use the theme of thwarted amorous relations to make political statements. The differences in nationality and politics between the two male lovers—a Russian in the earlier work, a German who flees to West Berlin in the second—reflect shifts in the German Democratic Republic from its early orientation toward the Soviet Union to its increasing attraction to the West, an affinity that significantly contributed to the building of the Berlin Wall. In both cases a long-term romantic union is prevented by the loyalty of the female protagonist to East German socialism. Yet the thematic bias of socialist realism does not find a true parallel in Wolf's style, in which experiments with narrative voice and temporal layers point forward to her later work.

In the late 1960s and early 1970s a number of Wolf's short stories and short narratives make significant strides away from the doctrine of socialist realism, both thematically and formally. "Juninachmittag" (1967; "June Afternoon") takes as its point of departure a down-to-earth family scene in a garden but introduces into it elements that fly in the face of the socialist realist aesthetic. Moving even further away from this aesthetic, the stories that make up *Unter den Linden,* subtitled *Drei unwahrscheinliche Geschichten* (1974; Three Improbable Stories), experiment with the fantastic mode. The title story is a dream narrative whose portrayal of the famous boulevard blurs the boundary between wakeful description and dreamlike envisioning; the other two stories in the collection, "Neue Lebensansichten eines Katers" ("The New Life and Opinions of a Tomcat") and "Selbstversuch: Traktat zu einem Protokoll" ("Self-Experiment: Treatise on a Report"), are science fiction.

Other works from this period depart markedly from the socialist realist doctrine dictating loyalty to the regime. *Till Eulenspiegel* (1972), which Wolf wrote with her husband Gerhard Wolf as the screenplay for a film, transposes the folktale from the fourteenth to the sixteenth century, depicting the struggles between peasants and aristocrats and the religious corruption of the time as an indirect means of attacking flaws in East German society. Similarly, the short story "Kleiner Ausflug nach H." (1980; "A Little Outing to H.") critiques the cultural politics of the GDR by satirizing its literary doctrines, functionaries, and censors.

Both the stylistic and the thematic rejection of socialist realism find their most extensive manifestation in the novel that became one of the most influential works in East German literature, *Nachdenken über Christa T.* Consisting of a first-person narrator's "re-creation" of her deceased friend Christa T. with the aid of letters, diaries, and sketches left behind, the narrative unmistakably criticizes the state's molding of a human being according to its conformist precepts. Perhaps even more radical was Wolf's replacement of the socialist realist emphasis on external reality and its ability to be documented with an attention to psychological nuance and an awareness that knowledge of other human beings can only be subjective and fragmentary. Exemplifying a multifaceted rejection of binary thinking, the novel employs an array of stylistic techniques that ally it with Western modernist fiction, rather than with the doctrinaire aesthetic program of socialism: lyricism, montage, interior monologue, and multiple temporal levels.

Nachdenken über Christa T. is exemplary of Wolf's notion of "subjective authenticity," the term she coined to define the "search for a new method of writing which does justice" to the "different reality" generated by self-confrontational writing.[6] As such, this novel, which represents a crucial turning point in GDR literature, is akin to what came in West Germany to be termed "new subjectivity." Not surprisingly, it has been one of Wolf's best-received works in the West, where it has served many readers as an entrée to her work.

The short story "Blickwechsel" (1970; "Exchanging Glances"), which depicts a scene in the lives of refugees fleeing the Red Army at the end of the war, looks ahead in microcosmic form to Wolf's voluminous autobiographical novel *Kindheitsmuster* (1976). Veiled portrayals of the author's experiences with national socialism, war, and flight to the West from her childhood in the 1930s until 1947, these texts exemplify the process of coming to terms with the past in which German intellectuals in both West and East were engaged during the postwar decades. This process was in some ways more difficult for writers in the GDR than for those in the Federal Republic because of the degree to which East Germany viewed its association with fascism as terminated by socialism. Hence one finds West German writers like Günter Grass, Heinrich Böll, Rolf Hochhuth, and Peter Weiss attempting to come to terms with Germany's problematic past before East Germans are able to broach the subject. What distinguishes Wolf's participation in this endeavor from the work of many of her fellow writers is her concern not only with the past per se but also with the question of how these past experiences helped shape the adult she became, an interest reflected in the novel's alternation between narration of the past and references to the narrator's present as well as to an intervening period in 1971.

In part through the influence of Anna Seghers, who functioned in many ways as a model for Wolf, Wolf became avidly interested in the writers and cultural milieu of German romanticism. The enthusiastic reception, (re)publishing, and reworking of romantic authors by East German writers during the 1970s is in part motivated by the numerous parallels between the situations of Germans in the Napoleonic era and in the GDR, both suffering under political and social oppression and the loss of autonomy, in particular the suppression of free speech. Yet, although this feature of Wolf's oeuvre represents another tendency shared by many of her colleagues in the GDR, in her case it is informed and enriched by her training in German literature. In her story "Neue Lebensansichten eines Katers," a satiric science-fiction response to

E.T.A. Hoffmann's similarly titled novel, the part of the feline author is assumed by a tomcat writing about his master, a professor who is using cybernetics and computers to seek the key to total human health and happiness. For Wolf, this kind of emphasis on rational faculties to the detriment of the affective realm can only prove misguided.

Yet an imbalance in the other direction can also be precarious, as Wolf shows in *Kein Ort. Nirgends* (1979; *No Place on Earth*), in which she imagines an encounter between the romantic writers Heinrich von Kleist and Karoline von Günderrode. As with many of her other texts, Wolf's interweaving of actual literary, biographical, and historical material into her fictionalized portrayal serves to underline the subjective nature of our perceptions of others and the complex elusiveness of human identity. In this instance, the psychological vulnerability and radical sense of alienation of the two writers, both of whose lives ended in suicide, stand as an extreme analogue to the disillusionment and depression Wolf herself experienced in the face of the growing rigidity of the totalitarian regime under which she lived, epitomized in the expatriation of protest singer Wolf Biermann in 1976.

After signing a document protesting the government's expulsion of Biermann, Wolf felt increasingly distanced from the regime and found herself in a position of growing disfavor; she was, for example, dismissed the same year from the executive committee of the Berlin chapter of the Writers' Union. Whereas many of her like-minded colleagues and compatriots left the GDR for the West during the politically difficult years that followed, Wolf remained to the bitter end, taking recourse in literature. Above all, she continued and extended her reading of feminist theory and women writers—older writers like the romantics Günderrode and Bettine von Arnim or the Biedermeier poet Annette von Droste-Hülshoff; more recent authors such as Marie Luise Kaschnitz, Marieluise Fleisser, and Ingeborg Bachmann; GDR colleagues such as Anna Seghers, Maxie Wander, Sarah Kirsch, and Irmtraud Morgner; and foreign writers like Virginia Woolf.[7] Wolf appears to be looking to women artists for alternative ways of viewing the world, for modes of living that allow men and women to coexist peacefully and humanely. This ideal is posited in much of her work in the 1970s and early 1980s, which takes an increasingly feminist turn.

Wolf's contributions to literary feminism cover a temporal spectrum ranging from the days of ancient Troy to the end of the twentieth century. Set some 20 years after it was written, "Selbstversuch" is a futuristic second-person narrative in which a woman scientist who has undergone a sex-change experiment explains to the professor who conceived it and with whom she had been in love why she broke off the experiment before her transformation to a man was complete. Gradually realizing that the professor is unable to love, the woman scientist rejects masculinity and truly comes into her own as a narrating subject and as a woman. This brief but dense story has much to say about the relationship of gender both to science and to the realm of emotional expression.

Very different in tone is the interior monologue *Kassandra* (1983; *Cassandra*), in which Wolf imagines the thoughts of the Trojan prophetess after Agamemnon takes her back to Mycenae following the fall of Troy. In selecting ancient Troy as the setting of her narrative, Wolf highlights a civilization in which patriarchy was at its height, one that was celebrated and commemorated in heroic epics that lie at the foundation of the Western literary tradition. Through Cassandra's associative memories, fantasies, dreams, and narrations centered around the Trojan War, Wolf offers a powerful critique of one of patriarchy's most destructive institutions. The narrative is accompanied by four essays in which Wolf expands on the story and its title character and makes important statements about women's status and women's writings.

Surveying Wolf's work from 1961 on, one makes an intriguing discovery: the locale treated recedes increasingly into the historical past. *Moskauer Novelle* and *Der geteilte Himmel* deal with contemporary East Germany; *Nachdenken über Christa T.* spans a period beginning in 1945 and extending to 1964; *Kindheitsmuster* depicts the autobiographical protagonist's childhood during the Third Reich; *Kein Ort. Nirgends* is set in the German romantic period, the early nineteenth century; and *Kassandra* moves back three thousand years to portray the fall of Troy. It is as if Wolf felt that by digging ever further back in history, she could discover something about herself and her society.

In her next major work, the narrative *Störfall: Nachrichten eines Tages* (1987; *Accident: A Day's News*), Wolf returns to the present-day German Democratic Republic, where her literary and political attention remains focused for the next several years. This work reflects Wolf's growing concern with world peace and with the serious threat posed to it by the nuclear arms race. In *Störfall,* the narrator's reactions to the 1986 nuclear accident at Chernobyl intermingle with thoughts about an operation on her brother's brain, occurring on the same day the reactor accident becomes public in East Germany. Some of the dominant themes of Wolf's oeuvre find their culmination: the inextricability of the private and the public; the potentially destructive effects of science, technology, and other products of rational thinking; and the emotional realm as a counterpoint to these forces. Yet the fact that technology makes possible the removal of a malignant tumor from the brain of the narrator's brother demonstrates Wolf's tendency to avoid one-sided biases and black-white dichotomies in favor of dialogue and a dialectical give-and-take.

Wolf has been one of the most celebrated writers of the German Democratic Republic, having over the course of her career been awarded the Artists' Prize of the City of Halle, the Heinrich Mann Prize of the Academy of Arts of the GDR, the National Prize Third Class of the Academy of Arts of the GDR, the Wilhelm Raabe Prize of the City of Braunschweig, the Theodor Fontane Prize for Art and Literature, the Literature Prize of the City of Bremen, the Georg Büchner Prize of the German Academy for Language and Literature, the Schiller Prize, the Franz Nabl Prize of the City of Graz, the Austrian National Prize for European Literature, the National Prize First Class of the GDR for Art and Literature, honorary doctorates from several universities, the Geschwister Scholl Prize in Munich, the Premio Mondello in Palermo, the Officier de l'Ordre des Arts et des Lettres in Paris, the Rahel Varnhagen von Ense Medal of the City of Berlin, and honorary membership in the American Academy and Institute of Arts and Letters, as well as a number of guest professorships and fellowships in the United States and elsewhere. Especially given this widespread recognition in both West and East, it is striking and disturbing that Wolf has suffered a double fall from grace since the elimination of the Berlin Wall. The first controversy surrounding her, carried on for the most part in the West German media, was launched by the publication of her narrative *Was bleibt* (1990; *What Remains*), the autobiographical story of a woman writer who is watched and shadowed by the State Security Service or Secret Police (Stasi). The second offensive followed the revelations in 1993 that Wolf had herself supplied information to the Stasi between 1959 and 1962. The last chapter of this volume will assess these seemingly contradictory episodes, including a discussion of the illuminating relationship of Wolf's narrative *Sommerstück* (1989; Summer Play), published before but written after *Was bleibt,* to the controversial narrative. Finally we will take a look at *Medea: Stimmen* (1996; *Medea: A Modern Retelling*) to study the ways in which the author again transforms an ancient myth to comment on contemporary social and political issues.

Chapter Two
Socialist Realism

The Doctrine

Because the first phase of Wolf's literary production was shaped by the doctrine of socialist realism, it will be helpful to survey the background of this political and aesthetic program as it was conceived in the Soviet Union and adopted in the GDR and other East Bloc countries following the war. The theory of socialist realism has its roots in Marxist writings and can be traced back to the turn of the century. Like Marxist thought in general, the theory of socialist realism received a major impetus for its development following the Russian Revolution of 1917. From 1928 to 1931 the Soviet Union experienced a kind of cultural revolution, a turbulent period that sought to overthrow old institutions, glorify politics, and celebrate the working class.

One result of this upheaval was a government decree in 1932 announcing that artistic and literary organizations in the Soviet Union would be dissolved and restructured. As a major part of this effort, it was hoped that instituting a systematic program of socialist realism would help restore order.[1] The term "socialist realism" first appeared in print on 23 May 1932 in *Literaturnaia Gazeta* (The Literary Newspaper) (Robin, 39); the doctrine was worked out in numerous discussions between 1932 and 1934 at plenary sessions of the organizational committee designed to establish the new Writers' Union. At the First Soviet Writers' Congress in August 1934, socialist realism was adopted as the official literary method for all Soviet writers.

As George Buehler points out, socialist realism did not grow organically from the literary environment but was "quite simply the product of political fiat." Stalin himself was involved in planning the systematization of the doctrine; he wanted it to be called "communist realism" but was persuaded that this was premature. Stalin's conception of the writer as the "engineer of the human soul" was reflected in the founding, at the request of the state, of the Soviet Writers' Association, designed to monitor the output of writers and to take action against those who did not conform to party politics.[2]

The concept of socialist realism has been confused since the term's first appearance. As Régine Robin notes, distinctions between the author's point of view, his or her political and social position, and the text itself, not to mention themes within the text, have tended to be blurred (39). The 1930s saw endless discussions about realism and verisimilitude, about whether socialist realism is a style, a method, a form, or a thematics. But the crucial distinction between the nineteenth-century social realism of a Stendhal, a Balzac, or a Flaubert and socialist realism lies in the fact that the latter is dialectical, active; it has a specific goal, orientation, or objective. This feature is well captured in the statement by the Soviet intellectual Nikolai Bukharin that socialist realism is engaged in translating the philosophy of dialectical materialism "into the language of art" (quoted by Robin, 72), a formulation reflecting socialist realism's debt to Engels and Lenin as well as to Marx. Socialist realism is intensely didactic, intended to educate the masses. The desire to appeal to all classes and types of people requires that socialist realists employ simple styles. The viewpoint from which the socialist realist narrates is that of the victory of socialism over capitalism, hence furthering the evolution from bourgeois capitalism to socialism to communism. Socialist realism seeks to depict not fragments but the totality of social relationships.

Just as Soviet socialist realism resulted from the transition from Czarist Russia to communism, socialist realism was adopted in the GDR to facilitate the transition from fascism to communism after World War II. The German Writers' Union was formed for the same reasons as its counterpart in the Soviet Union—to serve as a conduit for decrees from the SED (Socialist Unity Party) to the writers, to plan the (socialist realist) direction of literature in the GDR, and to control the literary output of its members (Buehler, 42). From the founding of the GDR in 1949 the arts were expected to serve state politics, and the socialist realist writer was to function as a comrade in arms for the state government or, in the formulation of the writer Johannes R. Becher, as a "tool for transformation" (quoted by Buehler, 10–11).

Socialist realism was introduced into the GDR at the first conference of the German Writers' Union in October 1947 and followed the example of its Soviet counterpart. A list of the major characteristics of socialist realism as practiced in the GDR, adapted from Buehler (45–64), provides a set of criteria to assess Wolf's early works.

1. Objective reflection of reality. This feature is not to be confused with realism or naturalism but rather requires "the union of truthful representation and of the ideological transformation of individuals" (Robin, 60). Socialist realism deals with historical processes, history being conceived of above all as class struggle. Socialist realist literature endeavors to portray reality in its revolutionary development toward communism; it anticipates the society of the future and incites the reader to become actively involved.

2. Partiality, or party orientation. The theoretical basis of this feature can be traced back to Lenin. The writer's paramount commitment must be to his or her class and party. The interests of socialism must take precedence over personal concerns.

3. National orientation or *Volkstümlichkeit* (folk character). Socialist realism must be rooted in folklore and "renewed by the progressive aspect of an optimistic and transformed folklore" (Robin, 63). The socialist realist text must take account of the political composition of society and portray the spirit of the people and country. Its themes should have nationwide implications and be in the best alleged interest of the state, and, above all, possess a broad appeal and be comprehensible to a wide spectrum of people. Socialist realism caters specifically to the cultural needs of the working class; at its heart is the struggle of the proletariat, the "new man" (Robin, 60).

4. The typical. This aspect of socialist realism was especially venerated by Engels and Lenin. It is well summarized in a passage from *Zur Theorie des sozialistischen Realismus* (On the Theory of Socialist Realism): "We regard typification as an artistic method of generalizing that aims at objective truth and that emphasizes and expresses in a manner that is artistically convincing the social in the individual, the general in the particular, the lawful in the coincidental, the whole (or the relation to the social whole) in the part, the (historically and socially) essential in concrete phenomena."[3] The types presented by socialist realist texts are intended to connote so-called universal truths.

5. The positive hero. The glorification of the hero who actively strives for the establishment of the socialist society may well be the most distinguishing characteristic of socialist realist literature. Advocated in particular by Maxim Gorky, one of the leading theorists and founders of socialist realism, the positive hero originally played an important role in supporting the process of collectivization in Russian agriculture. In the GDR, the positive hero of socialist realism is oblivious to personal sacrifice in his concern with the common good within the new socialist order and is meant to motivate the transformation among citizens to a similar socialist personality who is in harmony with himself and with society.

In a striking formulation Buehler observes that, "if one were to strip all of the political ramifications from socialist realism literature, the remaining characteristics of the positive hero in the service of mankind are strikingly reminiscent of the ideals espoused by Lessing, Schiller and Goethe" (27). As this passage suggests, the philosophy at the center of socialist realism is one of socialist humanism. Hence it is not surprising that socialist realism does not preclude romanticism, as long as it serves a mobilizing, progressive function; dreams and visions of the future are not prohibited, but the romanticism must be "revolutionary," as characterized by Andrei Zhdanov, Stalin's Minister of Culture (Robin, 61).

In other words, the doctrine of socialist realism ascribes a political function—the promotion of socialism—even to dreams and visions. Régine Robin offers a forceful critique of socialist realism. It is for her an "impossible aesthetic" because of "that totally insane dream of explicitly fashioning the social imaginary and what must be called—even apart from the conceptual framework of a Jung—the collective unconscious of a society or the zeitgeist of an era" (74). She argues that the unconscious cannot be "socially governed," and even goes so far as to claim that this kind of hindrance to the development of the social imaginary is a "clear symptom of a diseased society" (xxxi).

Yet it is precisely this free play of imagination, with its ability to reveal the abysses of the human soul as well as the heights, that socialist realism views as potentially pathological or "diseased." Exactly this fear motivates the opposition of socialist realism to modernism as a philosophical and aesthetic concept. Modernist literature, which explores the theme of despair and often depicts human beings as mediocre and lacking in faith, is anathema to socialist realism's celebration of the positive, exemplary hero who epitomizes loyalty to the socialist state. Modernism's attention to subjectivity and perspectivism, manifested stylistically in narrative modes like the internal monologue or stream of consciousness, can only be seen to undermine the socialist realist commitment to truthfulness and the portrayal of objective reality.[4] The two poles of socialist realism and modernism span a useful spectrum of evaluative criteria that are illuminating in reading Wolf's first two works of fiction.

Moskauer Novelle

In *Moskauer Novelle* (1961; Moscow Novella) Christa Wolf first tries her hand at a full-length work of fiction, having up to this time worked primarily as a critic and editor. The novella focuses on the East German pediatrician Vera Brauer, who on the eve of her thirtieth birthday in 1959 travels from East Berlin to Moscow with a delegation of Germans for a three-week medical technology conference. Their goal is long-term cooperation between the medical faculties of East Berlin and Moscow. While in Moscow Vera runs into Pavel Koschkin, a Russian serving as interpreter for the group, whom she had been close to for six months at the end of the war, when she was working as a clerk for the mayor of her village and he was a lieutenant for the occupying Red Army unit. Both are now married to others.

As is gradually revealed, Pavel is working as a translator and interpreter rather than as a doctor, as he had originally hoped, because of eye injuries sustained in 1945 in Vera's village while rescuing her brother from a burning Soviet munitions storehouse. Because it had been set on fire by two former Nazis whose subversive activities were known to Vera, she feels complicit in their guilt and hence in its outcome for Pavel, which she learns of only in the course of her present encounter with him, some fourteen years following the incident. Despite the strong attraction between them and despite Pavel's urgings, the two become only briefly involved in 1959.

Moskauer Novelle, conforming in many ways to the dictates of socialist realism, reflects the moment of Christa Wolf's strongest, most unambivalent commitment to the socialism that underlay the founding of the GDR in 1949. The text is certainly realistic in the classic, nineteenth-century sense. As in many novels of the last century, in the first paragraph of the narrative the reader is given details of place, time, and personage. Decor, as of Vera's hotel room in Moscow, is graphically evoked: "Massive armchairs with protective white covers, plush, dark blue curtains, lace doilies on the bed, a lamp with a purple silk shade, marble writing implements, and a crystal water decanter."[5]

Realistic details of daily life in Moscow abound. The narrator describes a rainy evening after midnight as follows: "At this late hour Moscow seemed to have decided to travel. Entire families poured out of the taxis that stopped every minute in front of the wide staircase, grandmothers, infants wrapped in blankets, with suitcases, boxes, and bundles. Groups of city-dwellers on their way to the country shoved their way more dexterously between broad peasant faces beneath white scarves or peaked caps. Islands of various nationalities surfaced above the stream; Tartar caps and colorful shawls, turned-up and drooping mustaches, full, flowery skirts above leather boots. White, yellowish, brown faces. All peoples of the huge country met here, the envoys of Moscow traveled in all directions" (*MN,* 14). Wolf endeavors throughout to give her reader a sense of Moscow's local color, from the lukewarm tartness of the kvass that Vera and her medical colleagues drink on the streets of the city to the wild gesticulations of a traffic attendant as they miss their bus.

Similarly, the narrator informs us about the main characters' ages and keeps careful track of the passage of time. Furthermore, the leitmotiv, which helps give cohesion to the realist fiction of Dickens, Thomas Mann, and many others, makes its appearance here in Pavel's green eyeglasses, a tag with rich associations that the reader identifies with him every time it recurs in the text. The realism of *Moskauer Novelle* is one of the features that makes it widely accessible, an important criterion in the socialist realist aesthetic.

Other elements more specifically reflect the "partiality" or commitment to socialism that motivates the doctrine under discussion. Vera calls Pavel "comrade" and sometimes speaks Russian with him, details that suggest socialist solidarity; his mention of Lenin (*MN,* 34) seems to have a similar function. The text contains several allusions to fascism, all negative. One of the more memorable instances occurs at a party where Vera encounters a Russian nurse in tears and learns that German fascists had hanged her father; this occasion provides one of the first opportunities for the reader to learn of Vera's feelings of guilt for the fact that she is German and that her father was a soldier in the war.

A further sign of commitment to the party is the character of Dr. Lidia Vorochinova, renowned pediatrician and professor at Moscow University, a seasoned communist who gives Vera sage advice about Pavel late in the novella. But the power of the socialist collective over the individual is perhaps most clearly embodied in the figure of Walter Kernten, an old friend of Vera's who is leading the group of Germans on the trip to the Soviet Union. A longtime radical, he had been one of the earliest members of the Spartacus League and had later suffered internment in a Nazi concentration camp because of his communist activities. As Vera's first teacher at the party school and one who in her opinion lives his life according to his socialist teachings, Walter has assumed the role of second father to her. In one of the most moving scenes in the novella, Walter tells of how he and his comrades survived life in the concentration camp through their party solidarity, epitomized in the socialist song to which they mouthed the words silently so as not to provoke the guards. Casting such a sympathetic figure as the virtual incorporation of the party conscience makes a strong statement on behalf of socialism.

The folk character idealized in *Moskauer Novelle* is not that of the GDR but that of the Soviet Union. The most extended example of this tendency is found in the scene in which the German group takes part in a celebration on a farmer's collective outside Kiev. In the lusty and festive atmosphere of the party, boundaries of class, economic background, and nationality become blurred; Vera becomes friendly with Russian peasant girls who hug and kiss her and confide to her details of their love lives, and socialist songs are sung in Russian and German. The overall mood is one of socialist brotherliness. It is during the visit to Kiev that Vera and Pavel become involved, although their sexual relationship is only intimated.

The party in the country can be seen as a harbinger of the ideal socialism of the future as projected in a conversation members of the German group and their interpreter have during the train ride from Moscow to Kiev. Asked by Vera about the most important characteristic of the man of the future, Pavel responds: "Brotherliness. Openness. Not having to mistrust others. Not envying others their success, helping them bear their failures. Not having to hide one's weaknesses. Being able to tell the truth. Guilelessness, naiveté, kindness are no longer bad words. Being able to deal with life no longer means being able to be hypocritical" (MN, 53). Although this speech qualifies Pavel as a positive, even exemplary hero in the socialist realist sense, the qualities he outlines represent not so much the socialist humanism at the heart of socialist realism as a fairly apolitical humanism that points forward to the philosophy informing much of Wolf's later work.

Vera herself demonstrates many of the traits singled out by Pavel, for example on one occasion buying ice cream for a strange boy who does not have enough money for it and often manifesting a communal spirit. As a pediatrician she is presented as a productive member of society who subordinates her individual desires to the greater good. As soon as she feels an interest in Pavel after seeing him in Moscow, she determines to counteract it and armor herself by promising to write her husband in Germany every day and urging him to write her frequently as well. Following the transgressive interlude in Kiev she regains control, aware of her power over Pavel and of the fact that matters lie in her hands. Wolf indicates this awareness both directly and indirectly, as in the song Vera sings at the country festival outside Kiev:

> Let them murmur, love, let them murmur,
> I don't know what's happening to me,
> The brooks keep on murmuring,
> And none of them loses its way.
>
> (MN, 67)

Although Vera nearly loses control again when she is consumed by jealousy and obsessively follows a woman she thinks is Pavel's wife, she finally regains her grip and encourages Pavel to take a position in Siberia that would carry him (and the socialist state) further. She not only does not yield further to his tendernesses but, as Helen Fehervary puts it, "patches up his relationship to his wife, and teaches him the benefits of sublimation for the larger cause of humanity."[6] Pavel's progress away from Vera is evident in the fact that he brings his wife along to the airport to see Vera off; Vera's renewed commitment to marital harmony is symbolized by the repaired pearl necklace she gives to Pavel's wife, from which she (Vera) had earlier extracted one pearl in a bet with Pavel.

Especially insofar as marital fidelity can be seen to symbolize in microcosmic fashion the loyalty that holds together the socialist state, Vera emerges in the end as the major positive or exemplary hero of *Moskauer Novelle* and as one of the text's most striking socialist realist features. She embodies the very qualities that she had distinguished as most important for the socialist of the future—"strength of character, will-power" (*MN*, 53), ultimately acting in the "strict and uncompromising" manner that the elderly Lidia Vorochinova praises as typical of her own, early communist generation (*MN*, 88). Vera thus reflects Wolf's opinion, expressed in a speech given three years after the publication of *Moskauer Novelle*, that socialism is to be equated with reason, which is "the yardstick by which things are measured [in the GDR], the ideal in whose name things are praised or censured here."[7]

The novella's idealized conception of the socialist human being and the spirit of a new and better socialist future it envisions led to a decidedly positive critical reaction in the GDR, manifested above all in Wolf's receipt of the Artists' Prize of the City of Halle.[8] The book was not published in the Federal Republic of Germany. In connection with Wolf's commitment to the socialist state in her early years of fiction-writing, certain passages of *Moskauer Novelle* take on enriched meaning when read in light of our current knowledge that she worked as an informant to the State Security Service, or Secret Police (Stasi), for two and a half years between 1959 and 1962, or at precisely the time she was writing this novella: " 'It is really strange,' [Vera] once said to Pavel, 'how much we forget in life, forget on purpose, if I can put it that way. And how demanding it is,' she added with a forced smile, 'how very demanding it is, to remember' " (*MN*, 29). Given the fact that Wolf's cooperation with the Stasi remained hidden for more than 30 years—until her file came to light in January 1993—and given the difficulty she had recalling the details of her interaction with the Secret Police, such as the code name she had been assigned, the passage quoted above takes on truly prophetic significance.[9]

In many ways, then—in terms of its realistic aspects, its support for the humanistic spirit of socialism, its idealization of the Russian peasantry, and its glorification of a positive socialist hero as typical of what the populace should strive for—*Moskauer Novelle* fulfills the program of socialist realism as handed down from the Soviet Union. In her 1973 essay "Über Sinn und Unsinn von Naivität" ("The Sense and Non-sense of Being Naive") Wolf criticizes the work as naive and "reminiscent of a political tract."[10] However, to call the work a "prime example" of socialist realism, as some critics have done, goes too far, because the text deviates in a number of ways from the dictates of the socialist realist aesthetic.[11] Perhaps most strikingly, the novella devotes considerably more attention to affairs of the heart than to political matters that were of interest at the time, such as class conflicts, details of industrial and agricultural production, and the welfare of the state. Not only is the progress of the romance between Vera and Pavel tracked in close detail, complete with blushes, loss of appetite, and restless nights; through Vera's eyes we follow the flirtations and amorous longings of others in the novella as well. The sphere of love, not work, receives the lion's share of Wolf's attention here. Sonja Hilzinger's comment on the projected vision of the new socialist human being, which she feels Vera and Pavel come close to realizing in the peasant idyll outside of Kiev, could apply to much of the novella: "This vision cannot last because it contains too much romantic idyll and too little relation to social reality."[12]

Running similarly against the grain of the socialist realist aesthetic is the narrative technique of the novella. In contrast to the third-person, omniscient perspective advocated by socialist realism, much of the narration here occurs in the form of narrated monologue, or the use of the third person to convey the thoughts of a specific figure, from inside the character's head, as it were. A few examples will illustrate the technique: "Early in the morning of the second day [Vera] wrote a long letter to her husband and mentioned seeing Pavel again. The casualness with which she handled it was already half a lie" (*MN,* 17); "Pavel's window was dark. Was he sleeping? Was he sitting in the hotel lobby? Was he possibly walking through the city?" (*MN,* 73); "[Vera] tore up the letter to her husband. [Pavel] didn't want to call me and had to do it anyway. I don't want to think about him, and yet I have to and have to. This desire is stronger than everything else. What should I do?" (*MN,* 43).

These passages, indicating not spoken dialogue but thoughts and demonstrating a progression from third-person external narration of Vera's thoughts to third-person internal narration to first-person narration of her thoughts or internal monologue, suggest that Wolf is moving away from the belief in a common language and viewpoint espoused by socialist realism and toward a stream-of-consciousness technique that is anathema to the socialist realist aesthetic. Other stylistic devices typical of modernism and eschewed by socialist realism include the use of fragmentary flashbacks to the past and of impressionistic description. The past relationship between Vera and Pavel is not narrated all at once but bit by bit, the way we actually remember. Both their relationship from 1945 and their second encounter in the present are not described as much as intimated, so that much is left to the imagination of the reader. When scenes are filled out in some detail, the detail is often impressionistically conveyed and reflective of inner experience. A typical example occurs during a scene on the way back to Moscow following a festive meal at a provincial hospital in the country at which Vera has been reminded of the guilt of her fascist German countrymen during the war: "They stopped for a rest at the edge of a small, sunlit wood. Vera lay down beneath a birch tree at a considerable distance from the others and stared at the sky, which was still blue even though the sun was already low on the horizon. Gradually the crystal-clear dome turned apple-green at the edges. A lake whose bottom she could not see. Black hour. Darkness above the waters. And it is not growing any lighter" (*MN*, 27).

Further thwarting the ideal of objectivity so crucial to socialist realism, the narrator sometimes offers her opinions on things, for instance the proper age to marry. Also striking is the sentimental, slightly saccharine tone that occasionally pervades the text, such as in the following examples: "[Vera] walked and looked and learned and talked and laughed and moved and rotated and rotated on a humming wheel that she hoped would never stand still. Until it did stop, with a jolt, so that it was suddenly deathly quiet and the only sound was her heart beating" (*MN*, 21); "Gaiety burst on the scene like a champagne cork" (*MN*, 24); "[Vera and Pavel] walked along the banks of the Moskva in the mild evening air. Stars burst open in the ink-blue sky, one after the other, and the headlights of the steamships on the water answered them in a brotherly fashion" (*MN*, 30). Passages like these do not appear to serve the progressive or revolutionary function that in the socialist realist aesthetic justified the use of romanticism.

A final feature that should be mentioned as atypical of socialist realism is the novella's autobiographical foundation. Like Christa Wolf, Vera turns 30 in 1959; we learn that at the end of the war Vera fled before advancing Soviet troops from the far reaches of the German Reich to a village in Mecklenburg, as did Wolf, and that she worked as a clerk for the mayor of that village, again like Wolf. In the opinion of Anna Kuhn, the autobiographical memories emerge as the "least contrived" passages of *Moskauer Novelle*.[13] This observation is significant. It points to the fact that, despite the novella's paradigmatic socialist realist elements, we perceive signs of very different developments to come, which were to overthrow the Soviet-based doctrine and move East German literature, metaphorically speaking, toward the West. Already here, in her first work of fiction, Wolf begins to manifest her dual status as paragon and rebel.

Der geteilte Himmel

The plot similarities between *Moskauer Novelle* and *Der geteilte Himmel* (1963; *Divided Heaven*) are obvious and have often been noted. The latter work appears to be even more of a Romeo-and-Juliet tale than is *Moskauer Novelle*, since not only geographical but also political differences separate the lovers. Rita Seidel is a young student at a teacher's training college in a large, industrial East German city who works during vacations in a railroad car factory. She has a two-year relationship with Manfred Herrfurth, a chemist ten years older than herself who travels to West Berlin for a conference and decides to remain in the West because of professional advantages. Although Rita visits him there, she chooses to return to the East, and shortly afterward the lovers are divided by the building of the Berlin Wall in August 1961. In despair, Rita is injured when she "falls" between two colliding railroad cars. The bulk of the narrative consists of her thoughts and recollections as she lies convalescing in a sanatorium.

Der geteilte Himmel clearly struck a chord in Wolf's readership, and not only in the divided Germany. The book made her famous overnight, becoming a bestseller that went into ten editions and sold 160,000 copies within a few months. It was soon translated into Polish, Russian, Hungarian, Bulgarian, Croatian, Serbian, Finnish, English, French, Spanish, and Japanese, and for it Wolf was awarded the GDR's most prestigious literary award, the Heinrich Mann Prize of the Academy of Arts.[14] To determine why *Der geteilte Himmel* has been called Wolf's "breakthrough" as a writer,[15] we will compare it with *Moskauer Novelle*, to look in particular at the way the later work also takes socialist realism as its point of departure but does not adhere to the doctrine consistently. Here too we encounter a conventional realist beginning that immediately identifies the protagonist and situates the narrative temporally and spatially; frequent references to time orient the reader chronologically throughout. However, *Der geteilte Himmel* contains many more references to contemporary events and politics than does *Moskauer Novelle*. For example, *Der geteilte Himmel* acknowledges and highlights the first time the Russians send a man into space—12 April 1961—by previewing it several times as "the news" before announcing it.[16] The text makes references to the Second World War and concomitant historical developments, above all, to the tensions throughout Germany in the early 1960s, the years just prior to and following the building of the Wall. Similarly, we find allusions to the desirability of goods from the West, to the superiority of West German science and technology, and to the flight of East Germans to the West, the problem that eventually compelled East German politicians to build the Berlin Wall.

Manfred's rhetorical question to an associate of Rita's at the railroad car factory could hardly be more pertinent: "We are, to put it simply, the political generation, right?" (*GH*, 68). The claim Manfred's father makes to Rita after she returns from West Berlin rather than staying with his son—that in [Herr Herrfurth's] day love was more romantic, and more absolute (*GH*, 192)—is undoubtedly to be taken ironically, in light of our knowledge of his infidelities and weak character. Yet there is some truth in the suggestion that, in the Germany of 1961, even the most personal of relations cannot remain untouched by politics. Rita's dilemma, when she is faced with the inhumane choice between her lover in the West and her socialist fatherland, individualizes a problem that affected thousands and makes concrete the looming presence of the Wall that divided a country from itself.

With regard to the element of partiality or party solidarity as well, *Der geteilte Himmel* offers a more varied and diverse range of possibilities than does *Moskauer Novelle*. The fact that Rita—a student, training to be a teacher—works in a factory reflects Wolf's own participation in the so-called Bitterfeld Movement. The East German government had called earlier for solidarity between intellectuals and workers as a means of fostering the spirit of socialism, but the program was officially launched at a conference in the industrial town of Bitterfeld in 1959; a second conference followed there in 1964. Intended to promote unity between intellectual workers and physical laborers, the movement adopted as its slogan, "Grab your pen, pal, the socialist national culture needs you!" For a time laborers organized into "Circles of Writing Workers" and published works of literature, and writers in turn took working-class jobs and documented their experiences in literary texts.

The setting of *Der geteilte Himmel* is clearly based on Halle, the large industrial city to which Wolf moved in 1959. Just as Wolf's decision to work in a railroad car factory there was motivated by her initial enthusiasm for the Bitterfeld policies, Rita is eager to absorb the lessons about labor and socialism that her position at the factory has to offer. From books and classes she moves to a world of work shifts, production norms, work brigades, overtime, rising and falling production, hiring, and layoffs. As in a bildungsroman, or novel of education, she learns about manifold aspects of socialism from a series of workers at the factory who take varying stances. Soon she feels completely at home in the factory, carries out her duties conscientiously, and fits well into her brigade or work group. The characterization of Rita's story as a "socialist education" is not only apt but points to one of the central socialist realist themes of *Der geteilte Himmel*.[17] The socialist spirit of life at the railroad car factory in general may perhaps be seen to culminate in the grand celebration held to commemorate the fifteenth anniversary of the factory's status as nationally owned.

Particularly as far as the factory sequences in *Der geteilte Himmel* are concerned, Wolf's early story "Dienstag, der 27. September" ("Tuesday, September 27") can be viewed as a sketch or study for the full-length narrative. Written in 1960 for the Soviet newspaper *Isvestia,* the story resembles an extended diary entry, as the title suggests, in which the first-person female narrator records the events of the day. These events include her attendance at a party group meeting of her brigade at the railroad car factory where she works. As in *Der geteilte Himmel,* this story is flavored with details of the feuds between workers at the factory, gossip about the workers and their families, and workers' conversations about life in a socialist brigade—conversations touching on surpluses and deficiencies in production, Lenin's views on work productivity, lack of profits, and the value of premiums.

The question in which these discussions culminate, "Are you a communist or an egotist?," encapsulates the alternatives as conceived by the population of East Germany in the early 1960s.[18] Precisely this question could be posed by Rita and Manfred, early incarnations of whom are sketched out in the "brigade story" (*GE,* 32) on which the narrator of

"Dienstag, der 27. September" is working. Although at this stage Manfred is called Robert, it is clear that Wolf is airing some of her difficulties with what was to become *Der geteilte Himmel* in this heavily autobiographical story. Foremost among the narrator's concerns is that the material—a girl working in a factory brigade whose boyfriend is a chemist—is banal; as the narrator muses, "I know that the real work will not begin until I have found the overarching idea that will make the banal subject matter both possible to tell and worth telling" (*GE,* 33). For Wolf, the "overarching idea" seems to have been the decision to tell the story of the lovers against the background of the increasingly divided Germany, since there is no doubt that in terms of pure narrative power, the political situation and the romantic relationship are mutually enriching.

As in *Moskauer Novelle,* in *Der geteilte Himmel* the positive features of socialism are set into further relief by contrast with fascism. In the later work the figure most closely associated with fascism is Manfred's father, who is revealed to have been a member of the *SA* (*Sturmabteilung,* or Storm Troopers) and to have compelled Manfred to join the Hitler Youth; an opportunist who in the new, socialist state has joined the SED, Herr Herrfurth defends his past by claiming to have been a "fellow traveler" (*Mitläufer, GH,* 45). His questionable political views are paralleled by his personal behavior as an unfaithful husband and lamentable father who neglected and beat his son.

Negative traits like these, both political and personal, do not have the last word in the narrative, however, which closes with Rita's perceptions of the many small acts of kindness and friendliness going on in households she observes through windows as she walks home through the streets at dusk: "Here, a man watches his wife as she carries the dishes out of the room, and she doesn't notice how surprised and grateful his glance is. There, a woman lays her hand on her husband's shoulder. She hasn't done that for a long time, but at the right moment she feels that he needs it. . . . [Rita] sees how every evening an endless quantity of friendliness that was consumed during the day is produced anew" (*GH,* 199).

It is no accident that the depoliticized socialism, or humanism, with which *Der geteilte Himmel* closes is perceived by its protagonist Rita Seidel. Rita's status as a positive, exemplary hero in the socialist realist sense acquires a special coloration through its association with stereotypically feminine qualities: she is highly sensitive, full of sympathy, and deeply convinced of the necessity of love. Like Vera in *Moskauer Novelle,* she thinks often about the role and function of love and typically takes care that in any given situation, whether professional or personal, love not be neglected. On one occasion with Manfred she is brought to tears by the memory of a child longing for a balloon and not getting one. Her last act in the narrative (prior to the walk home) is one of kindness—a visit to a seriously ill coworker and an attempt to comfort his wife.

Far from clashing with the theory of socialism, these "feminine" qualities support it. Rita's feminine humanism and the socialist ethic are especially effectively brought together in the image she conceives when she sees a flashing light while staring out at the river one night when she and Manfred are awakened by a storm: "We are the lighthouse. Out there, at sea, is our little boat, sending calls for help. We're returning its signals" (GH, 80). Although not made with reference to this passage, Anna Kuhn's comment about the "convergence of Rita's perspective with the communal 'we' of the frame [of the narrative] [to indicate] that Rita has been included in the socialist community, that she is to be viewed as a full-fledged member of the GDR," can be seen to apply here as well.[19]

Rita's feminine socialist humanism is buttressed by a critique of capitalism. She expresses skepticism about the power of the individual, for example, thinking at one point, "Relying on oneself alone borders on arrogance" (GH, 163). In the same vein, she claims on another occasion, "If anybody asked me: I would prefer the man who makes mistakes without thinking of himself to the one who only cares about what's best for himself" (GH, 114). In like manner, she embodies perseverance, in contrast to the flightiness and lack of commitment associated with the West; when Manfred sees how exhausted she is at the end of the day and urges her to give up her teacher's training program, she responds, "I can't just quit" (GH, 33).

Rita's inclination for socialist humanism and antipathy for capitalist modes of thinking becomes most graphically evident when she travels to West Berlin to visit Manfred. The fact that she buys a round-trip ticket for the streetcar to the western part of the city is telling: she knows from the beginning she cannot remain. After returning to the East, Rita observes how foreign one feels in a country where the language is the same but so much else is different. But her most penetrating—and probably most famous—insight concerns her sense of the purpose, or purposelessness, of life in West Berlin: "But in the last analysis what matters is eating and drinking and clothing oneself and sleeping. Why did they eat? I asked myself. What did they do in their dream apartments? Where did they go in those huge cars, as wide as the street? And what did they think about in this city, before they fell asleep at night?" (*GH*, 173). Precisely these reactions, which echo those of Wolf herself on visiting West Germany during the early 1960s, were not uncommon among East Germans upon suddenly encountering the West when the Wall fell in 1989—before assimilation began.

Rita's alienation from West Berlin is made to parallel the growing alienation between herself and Manfred, a detail that gives the narrative a good deal of its richness, since the two states of disinclination—personal and political—reflect and reinforce each other. Just as socialist humanism is gendered through its association with conventionally feminine traits as embodied in Rita, Manfred manifests typically masculine characteristics that are often linked to bourgeois capitalism. He is as opposed to sentimentality and talking about feelings as Rita is in favor of these things, and he advocates individualism, personal initiative, and other qualities that are anathema to the socialist ethic.

Manfred and, by extension (because of his rhetoric), the West are associated with a lack of stability and control that those in the East are seen to possess because they need to; following his decision to emigrate to West Berlin he feels vaguely disappointed because he has not withstood the "pressure of the harder, more disciplined life" (*GH*, 181). Yet in a letter from West Berlin to a friend, he suggests that the source of this greater rigor is fear: "What is 'social order' supposed to mean when what it comes down to everywhere is the unhappiness and fear of the individual" (*GH*, 133). His cynicism and disillusionment transcend political differences, however; statements like the following point to existential anxieties: "Most human lives run alongside each other—parallel lines that meet only in infinity" (*GH*, 100).

Especially when one considers that Manfred belongs to Wolf's own generation, which had grown up beneath one totalitarian regime (fascism) and moved seamlessly into another (socialism), his cynical pronouncements about his "unheroic era" (*GH*, 150) are worth noting. One critic goes so far as to call him Rita's "skeptical alter ego."[20] And nothing has given more credence to Manfred's views than events in Germany since the elimination of the Wall in 1989: "People are not made for socialism. If they are forced into it, they will go through grotesque contortions until they're back where they belong: at the fattest trough" (*GH*, 180–81).

Hence we see that the plea for socialism incorporated in Rita is dialectically counterbalanced by a comparably compelling voice in Manfred.

But the socialist realist project of *Der geteilte Himmel* is undermined by other elements in the text as well. To a much greater extent than in *Moskauer Novelle*, the narrative technique thwarts the dictates of the socialist realist aesthetic. To be sure, Rita's narrative is framed by the introductory and concluding remarks of an omniscient narrator who speaks in the first-person plural and seems to represent the inhabitants of the city where she lives, like a voice of the people; this narrator occasionally breaks into the central story to make editorial remarks, notably at the beginning of 1961: "At that time we didn't know—no one knew—what kind of year lay ahead of us. A year of the most inexorable trials, not easy to endure. A historical year, as people will later say" (*GH,* 88).

However, because the bulk of the narrative consists of Rita's memories and thoughts as she lies convalescing in a sanatorium, it is not surprising that the story is conveyed largely from her point of view, thus contradicting the socialist realist demand for objectivity. At times the reader is taken directly into Rita's mind, a perspective conveyed by the use of the present or present perfect tense and hence similar to the stream-of-consciousness technique. Moreover, even more overtly than in *Moskauer Novelle*, the narrative is not linear, as would be the case in a conventionally realist text, but rather alternates between the predominantly past narration and occasional interruptions or intrusions from Rita's present life in the sanatorium. The following example demonstrates all three features: "September has passed. One night, unexpectedly, the fall rains begin. They fall steadily, forming a gray curtain in front of the sanatorium windows that does not lift for days" (*GH,* 62).

As in *Moskauer Novelle,* the socialist realist aesthetic is further undermined in *Der geteilte Himmel* by a tendency toward sentimentality. The following two passages are typical: "The little room with all its contents and its two residents [Rita and Manfred] became the gondola of a huge swing that was attached somewhere in the blue-black dome of the sky and that swung so smoothly and so high that they could only feel it move when they closed their eyes" (*GH,* 24); "[Rita's] thoughts wandered through her mind like swarms of clouds" (*GH,* 36). Finally, the autobiographical elements of the narrative, like those of *Moskauer Novelle,* run counter to the socialist realist criterion of objectivity.

All these features of *Der geteilte Himmel*—autobiographical echoes, intrusions of lyricism and sentimentality, as well as the departure from a third-person omniscient perspective, the rejection of linear narration, and other techniques that bring the text closer to modernist fiction than to socialist realism—caused Wolf difficulties and contributed to the extensive debates that occurred both orally and in the East German media over *Der geteilte Himmel;* as Alexander Stephan writes, "In the early '60s, flashbacks, memory monologues, and the abrupt confrontation of subjective-lyrical with critical-reflective passages were as discredited in the eyes of some Marxist critics as the topics of escaping the GDR, the building of the Wall, suicide, and nihilism."[21]

The last two themes Stephan lists bring us to a perhaps even more important way in which *Der geteilte Himmel* departs from the program of socialist realism and looks forward to much of Wolf's later work. Theodore Ziolkowski points out that a striking number of German novels written between 1959 and 1965 (such as Günter Grass's *Die Blechtrommel* [1959; *The Tin Drum*]) present the "view from the madhouse," although he does not mention Wolf.[22] Insofar as we learn near the end of *Der geteilte Himmel* that Rita's supposed accident was a suicide attempt and that her convalescence in a sanatorium is primarily a treatment for depression, Wolf's narrative can be seen as typical of modern literature's fascination with psychological illness and its ramifications— a topic eschewed by socialist realism. The passage in which Rita admits to herself that she did not attempt to move out of the path of the oncoming railroad cars contains another telling revelation: "[The cars] are coming right at me, she felt, and yet she also knew that she was making an attempt on her life. Unconsciously, she allowed herself one last attempt at flight—no longer because of despairing love, but rather because of despair at the fact that love, like everything else, is transitory" (*GH,* 190). In other words, Rita's suicidal accident is the result not only of her loss of Manfred, not only of insurmountable political differences between them (which parallel incompatibilities of character), but of an existential insight—despair at the transience of all human experience.

Sonja Hilzinger sees Rita's accident and subsequent convalescence as typical of a plot pattern in Wolf's fiction, consisting of the stages of personal crisis, mastery of the crisis, and (re)integration into socialist society, a process in which the crisis is overcome—as here—through narration.[23] While this generalization is accurate, I would argue that in *Der geteilte Himmel* this process is nonlinear and dialectical: certain aspects of Rita's commitment to socialism are stronger before her accident, following her socialist education at the factory, than afterwards, and despite her sense of reintegration after the accident, the existential despair that helped cause it lingers in the reader's memory as a distinct break with the politically based doctrine of socialist realism.

Belief in the socialist collective, on the one hand, awareness of the individual's existential isolation, on the other—in *Der geteilte Himmel* the two modes of seeing, both presented more compellingly than in *Moskauer Novelle,* dialectically counterbalance each other with relatively equal force. As we will see, in this regard *Der geteilte Himmel* represents a rare, if not unique, moment in Wolf's work.

Chapter Three
New Directions

Early Stories

The early stories "Dienstag, der 27. September" (1960; "Tuesday, September 27") and "Juninachmittag" (1967; "June Afternoon") are similar in mood and in the autobiographical framework they share: both are told by a first-person East German narrator who has intellectual interests as well as a family, a similarly intellectual husband and two small daughters. Both stories depict the narrator's everyday life—her tasks as a mother, her children's activities. There is no "plot" to speak of; both stories could best be characterized as vignettes. Even though the portrayal of domesticity is punctuated by more politically colored references to the GDR and to the situation of the divided Germany, the personal, quasi-idyllic tone and subject matter of these stories do not accord with the dictates of socialist realism.

As noted in chapter 2, "Dienstag, der 27. September," written for the Soviet newspaper *Isvestia,* can be seen as a preparatory sketch for *Der geteilte Himmel* in its attention to the narrator's job in a railroad car factory and to the concerns of the workers there. The earlier work resembles a diary entry, as the title suggests, in its focus on the details of the day being described, for example on the younger daughter's injured foot and her excited anticipation of her fourth birthday the following day. Yet we also learn that the narrator's husband is reading Lenin's *Letters to Gorky* and that the couple talks about the sovereignty of the individual in a socialist country—an issue that, in the year before the Berlin Wall was built, was even more pertinent than Wolf could guess at the time. Similarly, the child's injury turns out to be the point of departure for other political observations; when the narrator takes the girl to the doctor, she overhears other patients in the waiting room speculating about the differences between East and West Germany, the superiority of Western products, and the dependence of some East German citizens on compatriots in the West.

Alongside these political references, however, the story displays an interest in the minutiae of daily life and of what might be called life management that will become increasingly prevalent in the work of Christa Wolf. Three themes stand out:

    1. The business of living life, above all in the small increments of which it is composed. An observation the narrator makes near the end of "Dienstag, der 27. September" is typical of this concern: "Before going to sleep I think about the fact that life consists of days like these."[1]
    2. The activity of writing, which, though difficult, can give meaning and cohesion to the random events of everyday life.
    3. The importance of memory and its role in narration.

As we shall see, these themes will recur with rising frequency and significance in Wolf's subsequent works.

The setting of "Juninachmittag" is even more idyllic than that of "Dienstag, der 27. September," since the later story is set in the family garden. The paradisiacal associations that gardens typically have are heightened here by this garden's description as "the archetype of a garden. The garden incarnate" (*GE,* 34). As in "Dienstag, der 27. September," domestic life receives primary attention. The first-person narrator sits reading in the garden as her husband works in it; the scene is filled in with the small details the narrator observes—her younger child's sun-bleached hair, the movements of a snail the child observes, the creatures produced by cloud formations, the child's idiosyncratic pronunciation, the word games the family plays, the affection both daughters demonstrate for their mother, unpleasant neighbors.

As is often the case with Wolf, however, even seemingly trivial details can be endowed with meaning. A neighbor who complains about the possibility that flowers in the narrator's garden might develop into puffballs whose seeds would float over and fertilize his yard provides the opportunity for the narrator to make a satirically critical comment on excessive order and accuracy, reflecting Wolf's view that these traits threaten to stifle imagination and creativity.

While not lost, paradise in "Juninachmittag" is invaded by stories of mistreatment, murder, and fatal accidents recounted in newspapers and told by neighbors, as well as by allusions to the peculiar political situation of Germany at the time; the narrator mentions the helicopters flying along the border and observes that the planes heard above, apparently flying from east to west, are in fact flying from the West (West Berlin) to the West.

Like the narrator of "Dienstag, der 27. September," this narrator muses about the process of narration and its finished product. The story opens with such a speculation: "A story? Something firm, tangible, like a pot with two handles that you can grab hold of and drink from? Perhaps a vision, if you understand what I mean"(*GE*, 34). This passage hints at the two poles spanned by all fiction—reality and imagination. Since most of Wolf's works are strongly autobiographical, memory is often the force that mediates between the two poles.

Perhaps the most striking feature of the narrative technique in this story, evident in the passage quoted above, is the fact that the narrator addresses the reader, thereby engaging him/her in the narrative and calling self-conscious attention to the process of narration. This innovation in Wolf's work, which marks a clear break with the objectivity called for by socialist realism, will become a hallmark of her work. Margit Resch elaborates: "Every narrative technique practiced in 'June Afternoon' shall become a stroke in Wolf's literary signature: placing the narrator and other characters of the story in close autobiographical vicinity, a technique that emphasizes the subjectivity of the narrative perspective; making the narrator both object acting in the story and subject telling it, which imparts the illusion of authenticity; bearing witness to contemporary daily life punctuated by flashes of external threats . . . ; and, most crucially, involving the reader as arbitrator and commentator."[2]

Hence we see retrospectively that both "Dienstag, der 27. September" and "Juninachmittag," while perhaps not striking in themselves, function as a kind of testing ground for themes and stylistic devices that will characterize Wolf's later narratives. The theme of remembering, for example, is central to her best-known work, *Nachdenken über Christa T.* (1968; *The Quest for Christa T.*).

Nachdenken über Christa T.

In *Nachdenken über Christa T.* an unnamed first-person narrator attempts to reconstruct the life of her friend Christa T., who died at age 35 of leukemia, with the aid of her (the narrator's) memories and the papers Christa T. has left behind. The book had a torturous publication history. Although the first version was finished in 1965 and the second in 1967, the manuscript did not pass inspection by the censors. Wolf agreed to certain changes. In 1968 parts of the book were read on the radio in East Germany (DDR Rundfunk) and published in the GDR journal *Sinn und Form,* all of which served to whet the interest of potential readers of the narrative. But state officials continued to drag their feet. By the time the book actually appeared in 1969, demand in East Germany far exceeded supply. In the same year in West Germany, where reviews and publicity had also aroused great interest, Luchterhand was quick to publish and republish, and *Nachdenken über Christa T.* was soon a bestseller. (Because the copyright date originally established by the East German Mitteldeutscher Verlag was 1968, in the expectation that the book would be published that year, this date has been reprinted in subsequent East and West German editions, so that 1968 is usually given as the year of publication, although the work in its entirety did not see the light of day until 1969.)[3]

What was all the fuss about? Flying directly in the face of the doctrine of socialist realism, Christa T. represented to the censors a character who is "unfit for life" (*lebensuntüchtig*): although a valuable human being, she is too sensitive for life in a socialist society. As the authorities read it, *Nachdenken über Christa T.* implied that only those who conformed would survive in the GDR, and this implication disturbed them. They feared that the literary public was not yet ready, not mature enough, for such a message and such a character.

In order to understand the vehemence of the state resistance to Wolf's narrative, it is helpful to recognize the atmosphere in which she wrote it. The mid-1960s were years of renewed rigidity in the GDR, bringing reinforced attempts to discipline authors and critics. Leading up to these years were events such as the workers' uprising in East Berlin on 17 June 1953, which was put down by Soviet tanks; the revolution in Hungary in October 1956, which was dealt with in a similarly bloody fashion; and the construction of the Berlin Wall in August 1961; the revolt that followed in Prague in the spring of 1968 likewise fell to the military force of the Soviet regime.

Given the fear that Soviet actions in these events reveal, it is little wonder that censors in the GDR, acting in accordance with Soviet wishes, were uneasy about the publication of *Nachdenken über Christa T.* For Wolf's narrative wholly overturns the principles of objective narration and characterization on which the socialist realist aesthetic was based. Whereas realist or socialist realist writers are confident of their ability to draw a convincing character and of their readers' ability to believe in that character's fictional existence, Wolf's narrator again and again emphasizes the difficulty of knowing and hence recreating another human being, of conveying another person to readers. The English title—*The Quest for Christa T.*—is highly evocative of the process in which the narrator is engaged, since the motif of the quest, or the search for an external goal that usually possesses symbolic or spiritual significance, is an old one that has been found in virtually all cultures of all eras.[4] Feeling that Christa T. is "disappearing," the narrator wants to "think her further, make her live and grow old, as everyone has a right to do."[5]

Although the narrator has tangible documents to aid her in her quest—diary entries, letters, notes, manuscripts, sketches, observations, stories, and lists left behind by Christa T., and although the narrator has ultimate control in writing her narrative ("[Christa T.] moves when I want her to," 9), the narrator is aware of her inability to know what her subject actually thought on most occasions. The narrator can give us the bare facts: Christa T. was one year older than herself, became her classmate in 1944, later became a teacher, attended the university in Leipzig—"Four places of residence. Two occupations. One husband, three children. A trip. Illnesses, landscapes. A few people remain, a few are added" (*NCT,* 64).

Similarly, the narrative provides some facts, often indirect ones, about the historical period in which Christa T. lives. Significantly, the school the girls attend is called the Hermann Göring School; mention is made of a boy who is publicly praised for denouncing his father for listening to enemy radio stations; the narrator notes that, following the attempt to assassinate the Führer (on 22 July 1944), she and her schoolmates wear their Hitler Youth uniforms to show their unswerving loyalty to him. Later commenting on the postwar years in the GDR, the narrator writes, "At that time there were not many opportunities for us, not many choices of thoughts, hopes, or doubts" (*NCT,* 32). Similarly, the narrator mentions the night that she and Christa T. listen to Western radio reports of the battles in Budapest and hear between the lines "the loud, barely suppressed, scornful laughter over the failure of what had been called 'utopia' " (*NCT,* 132)—an elliptical allusion to the brutal quashing of the Hungarian revolution by Soviet troops in October 1956.

And yet the limitations of empirical knowledge are intimated by the rhetorical question the narrator finds among Christa T.'s notes, "But what are facts?" (*NCT,* 170). Within the fictional framework of the narrative, the difficulty of knowing another human being and of telling her story is compounded by three factors that are thematized in the text:

    1.   The unreliability of memory. At the outset of the narrative the narrator paradoxically observes that she must forget her memory of Christa T.: "Memory colors in a deceptive fashion" (*NCT,* 9).

   2. The inevitably subjective nature of perception. After writing about the principal of the school where Christa T. teaches, the narrator adds, "Perhaps the man, her principal, wasn't like this, but he could have been. We can't ask him; he is dead. But how should one ask him, even if he were alive? How should we know what image he would have had of himself and would choose to expose?" (*NCT,* 107).

   3. The narrator's tendency to identify with Christa T. At times she narrates Christa T.'s story so closely that the reader loses track of where the one figure stops and the other begins, especially because the narrator often compares her life with Christa T.'s and occasionally alternates between "she" and "I" in her narration. This factor is further complicated by the question of autobiography: to what extent is the narrator to be identified with Wolf herself, and to what extent should Christa T. be linked to someone Wolf actually knew? In Wolf's "Self-Interview," a dialogue about the narrative between the voices "Question" and "Answer" that was published in 1968 in the periodical *Kürbiskern,* "Answer" claims that both the narrator and Christa T. are invented.[6] As Christa Thomassen suggests, however, "Answer" identifies with the narrator of *Nachdenken über Christa T.* and hence should not be equated with Wolf but rather was created by her, so that the "Self-Interview" is also revealed to be a fiction.[7] Wolf's own statements suggest that Christa T. is both based on a real person and invented. Like most successful fictional characters, she is a composite of the actual and the imaginary.

   The epistemological skepticism, or thematization of the difficulty of knowing, in *Nachdenken über Christa T.* is paralleled by linguistic skepticism. Frustration and even despair over the inadequacy of verbal language in conveying experience is a prominent theme in German literature, especially from the late eighteenth century onward. Writers such as Friedrich Schlegel, Novalis, Heinrich von Kleist, Georg Büchner, Franz Grillparzer, Franz Kafka, and Hugo von Hofmannsthal, to mention only a few, call repeated attention to the insufficiencies of language as a medium of communication. Herself a former student of German literature who is thoroughly familiar with this tradition, Wolf creates in Christa T. and the narrator characters who are intensely aware of the pitfalls of language yet who also value its powers: as the above authors, along with many others, recognize, despite its shortcomings language is the only medium we have in which to write.

   The narrator claims that she has found a small book among Christa T.'s things with the following inscription, in a child's scrawl, on its cover: "I would like to write poetry and I also love stories" (*NCT,* 22). Yet Christa T. waits to begin writing. The narrator speculates that "She must have recognized early on that we are unable to tell things the way they are"; "She perceived that naming is rarely accurate and that a name only coincides for a brief time with the thing to which it is assigned" (*NCT,* 38, 40). The narrator relates that Christa T. is afraid of inexact, inappropriate words and believes that life can be "wounded" by words; hence it is not surprising that in the narrator's opinion she does not possess the "courage to invent" (*NCT,* 169–70; 81). A formulation of the narrator's sums up the awareness that she and Christa T. share: "You can't tell it the way it happened. But if you can tell it the way it was, then you weren't there, or the story happened a long time ago, so that it's easy to be impartial. However, the fact that you have to separate events and take them one after another in order to be able to narrate things that are in reality so intertwined as to be inexplicable . . . As far as I can see, this was always the case with her, Christa T." (*NCT,* 68).

And yet, in keeping with the ambivalence and paradox that typically characterize the phenomenon of linguistic skepticism, both Christa T. and the narrator write. The narrator finds poems and stories left behind by the subject of her narrative, as well as the exasperated exclamation, "To think that I can only get through life by writing!" (*NCT,* 39). And the narrator claims that "Writing means making things great" (*NCT,* 173). But her philosophy of composition eliminates some of the pressure that the realist method creates, since for her writing means "offering examples"; she claims not to have the "wonderful, uninhibited option of invented certainty" (*NCT,* 48). The liberating result of epistemological and linguistic skepticism is that it is not important whether a story "really" happened the way it is written—who can know, and who can tell?

This conception of writing is all-important for the style and structure of *Nachdenken über Christa T.* The narrative's quality was recognized even by those first exposed to it, the two readers who were asked to provide anonymous evaluations for the Mitteldeutscher Verlag, the press to whom Wolf submitted the manuscript in March 1967; one reader calls the manuscript a "linguistic masterpiece" even while rejecting it because of its depiction of the title figure.[8]

The text presents the reader with difficulties of chronology, plot, and character. Rather than being narrated in a linear, cause-effect fashion, from beginning to end, stories are often told partially, then broken off and continued at a later point. Memories from the narrator's school and university days with Christa T. interrupt the account of an event from their adulthood. Characters appear suddenly, without introduction, and reappear at a different stage of their lives, without transition. Motifs pop up and vanish again; it is up to the reader to perceive their connection to the narrative, since this is often not made explicit. Pieces of stories are fitted into the whole, in the manner of a collage or jigsaw puzzle, or written over existing stories, as in a palimpsest. For example, the narrator writes about Christa T.'s illness and death, then about her life, a pattern that recurs several times. One of the narrator's principles is that "chronology is disturbing" (*NCT,* 111)—a far cry from the narrative conventions that underlie the doctrines of both social realism and socialist realism.

For one accustomed to the laws of older narrative, in which an experience is related "as it actually was" (*NCT,* 49), reading Wolf's narrative requires some adjustments. Although the narrator points out that the fact that Christa T. really lived and died, for the most part unrecognized, is anything but invented, she emphasizes that her inability to know much else leads to a need for invention. The result is a narrative style that could be described as provisional: again and again she recounts an event or a conversation, then undermines its fictional veracity by adding, "maybe it happened this way, it might have happened differently," or words to that effect, thus putting into practice her theory of writing as the positing of examples. We recall Christa T.'s conversation with her school principal, cited earlier, where the uncertainty about knowing what was said is compounded by the difficulty of truly knowing another. Similarly, the narrator frequently notes that this figure or that has to be invented, thereby raising to the level of self-consciousness something that every reader of realist fiction is aware of but tends to forget in the act of reading.

Self-consciousness is only one of the features linking *Nachdenken über Christa T.* to postmodernist literature. Representing Wolf's hitherto most radical break with the aesthetics of socialist realism, the narrative marked an irrevocable turning point in East German literature. The epistemological and linguistic skepticism driving *Nachdenken über Christa T.* and its resulting multilayered, nonlinear style are all manifested in the narrator's attempt to recapture the title character. She is depicted throughout as one who does not toe the GDR line but steps over it, one who fails to conform. After arriving near the end of the war as a pupil in the class of the narrator, Christa T. refuses to act in a deferential manner to the teacher as the others do; by the same token, she is the sole pupil who gives flowers to an unpopular teacher, since this teacher is the only one who does not make her feel unfree and unhappy. As the narrator tells it, Christa T. once professed in class that she had no favorite subject but would rather go walking in the forest. The narrator sums up Christa

T.'s nonconformity by speculating, "It always seemed as if she had taken it upon herself to be everywhere at home and everywhere foreign, at home and foreign in the same second" (*NCT,* 19 –20).

Christa T.'s heightened sensitivity, which is one of the features the narrator comments on most frequently, is perhaps most graphically manifested in her abhorrence of violence and cruelty. Violence figures prominently in the "darker half of the world that she always wanted to escape" (*NCT,* 29), as the narrator puts it. Like a hypersensitive seismograph, Christa T. reacts with shock and sadness when an intoxicated farmer hurls her family's tomcat against a wall and kills it, when a magpie's eggs are smashed against a rock or its baby birds thrown against the wall of the barn, when one of her pupils bites off the head of a toad. Given Christa T.'s loathing of violence, it is not surprising that she feels instinctively cold toward Hitler, even before she understands him intellectually. This detail suggests that the smaller acts of gratuitous cruelty that so disturb Christa T. have larger, emblematic significance in terms of the Germany in which she lives.

Christa T.'s hatred of violence and sensitivity to the suffering of others are central to her humanistic philosophy of life. As the narrator imagines that Gertrud Dölling, a former professor of Christa T.'s, will formulate it, "She had only one interest: human beings" (*NCT,* 52). Asked while a university student what she wants to become, Christa T. replies, "A human being" (*NCT,* 40). Imagining a conversation between Christa T. and a young school principal with whom she had a relationship, the narrator hypothesizes that one of the questions Christa T. asked him was, "What does a human being need?" (*NCT,* 45), and she and the narrator share a fascination with the question, "What does the world need in order to become perfect?"—to which their answer is "absolute love" (*NCT,* 64).

Christa T.'s nonconformism, abhorrence of violence, and humanistic convictions are complemented by her antipathy to factual reality. The narrator concludes from notes Christa T. has left behind that "she did not want to come to terms with naked, true reality" (*NCT,* 110). Christa T. dreads the "new world of those without imagination. Of the fact people. Of the go-getters, as she called them" (*NCT,* 55). In the narrator's imagined conversation between the young school principal and Christa T., he tells her that she does not like it "when something is completely correct or completely in order" (*NCT,* 43).

Christa T.'s condition is unwittingly diagnosed by a former pupil of hers who runs into her years later while studying medicine; as the narrator imagines their conversation, he confidently claims, "The secret to good health is conformity" (NCT, 112). The significance of her noncon- formity in terms of this metaphor is clear, and her bad health manifests itself in a number of other ways as well. The narrator conjectures that Dr. Dölling would describe her as "at risk" (NCT, 51). Given the paral- lel, crucial to Moskauer Novelle, between marital fidelity and loyalty to the state, Christa T.'s affair with a hunting friend of her husband's reflects not only moral but ideological weakness.

In precise contrast to the active, positive hero of socialist realism, Christa T. is dreamy and passive. Her sense of impotence is reflected in her identification with the north German poet Theodor Storm, about whom she writes that "The conflict between desire and inability pushed him into life's corner" (NCT, 98). As Dr. Dölling in the narrator's con- ception would describe it, Christa T. is surrounded by a "sea of sadness," the result of people's failure to be the way she saw them (NCT, 53). In most graphic opposition to the positive hero celebrated by socialist real- ism, this state of mind even leads her to thoughts of suicide, as the nar- rator knows from a letter Christa T. has left in her diary.

The actual problem of this psychologically endangered protagonist, so new to East German literature, appears to be that "the game of varia- tions has ended" (NCT, 136), as Christa T. writes in a letter: now that she is the wife of a veterinarian, living in Mecklenburg, having children, certain things are set, no longer variable—a situation directly contra- dicting the narrator's revelation that "[Christa T.] didn't like things to be fixed" (NCT, 166). Just as this text, in its awareness of the elusive and dynamic nature of identity, repeatedly points to the difficulty of know- ing another person and suggests that this process is ongoing rather than a finite project; just as the narrator emphasizes the provisional nature of narration, which seeks not to give definitive accounts but to suggest possibilities, for Christa T. (and through her, for the narrator) life is, ide- ally, process, aimed not at conclusions, at fixed principles, at security and stability—which would be tantamount to stasis—but at a never- ending quest, consisting of self-exploration and self-discovery. Christa T. writes of the "long path to one's self that does not want to end" (NCT, 173); the narrator repeatedly mentions "the difficulty of saying 'I'," which is another way of advocating a dynamic rather than static exis- tence—pronouncing that pronoun suggests that we have become who we are and that we know what that is; and the epigraph to the entire narrative is a phrase by Johannes R. Becher, who became the East Ger- man minister of culture in 1954: "What is it: this coming-to-oneself?"

Although *Nachdenken über Christa T.* is in so many ways antithetical to the dictates of socialist realism, as Wolfram Mauser and Helmtrud Mauser point out, the concept of experience Wolf presents here does not merely open up the possibility of bypassing fossilized ideology but also possesses the power of breaking it down. In this way the work was intended to offer a constructive contribution to the progress of socialism in the GDR.[9] Possibly because the notion of "self" as presented in the text is so multilayered, dynamic, and complex, it could not be easily inserted into the dichotomy between "social" and "personal" that is central to East German literary interpretation, just as Christa T. cannot be categorized alongside the heroes of earlier works produced in the GDR. In a multitude of ways, *Nachdenken über Christa T.* represents not a search fulfilled but a new beginning.

Till Eulenspiegel

Wolf's next major work is on the surface quite different from *Nachdenken über Christa T.* Written together with her husband Gerhard as a screenplay for DEFA (East German Film Society, Inc.), *Till Eulenspiegel* was published in 1972 and produced as a film, directed by Rainer Simon, in 1975. The Wolfs' version is based on *Dyl Ulenspiegel,* a folktale published in 1515 and thought to have been written by the Low Saxon author Hermen or Hermann Bote. Although it cannot be definitively determined whether the title figure actually lived, evidence suggests that there was a Dyl Ulenspiegel and that he died in 1350. Bote's *Dyl* is composed of some eight dozen episodes, each consisting of a short comic story or *Schwank.* Such comic or farcical stories, often telling of a practical joke played on an opponent that demonstrates his stupidity and the cleverness and cunning of the joker, were enormously popular in sixteenth-century German literature. These short comic tales belong to the tradition of fool's literature so widespread at the time, which includes Sebastian Brant's *The Ship of Fools* (1494), Erasmus' *The Praise of Folly* (1511), and Thomas Murner's verse epic *Of the Great Lutheran Fool* (1522).[10]

Bote's Dyl, who has been called "Europe's most famous jester" (Oppenheimer, xxi), supremely exemplifies the type of the *Schalk,* the cunning joker or rogue figure who stands at the center of sixteenth-century comic prose writing, although the folktale is set in the fourteenth century. While merely a humble peasant, Ulenspiegel is an expert and unscrupulous role-player who tries out a variety of identities in his efforts to lie, cheat, and deceive others. In the course of his adventures he assumes the roles of painter, tailor, blacksmith, teacher, carpenter's apprentice, optician, launderer, cook, and barber, among other occupations.

In the relative ease with which Dyl Ulenspiegel succeeds in deceiving his victims, Bote mocks the folly and gullibility of particular groups or professions and even of human nature in general. Lampooned above all are the clergy; royalty and Jews are also favorite targets. A few episode titles will convey a sense of the objects and flavor of Bote's satire: "How Eulenspiegel, with a false confession, talked the priest of Kissenbrück out of his horse"; "How Eulenspiegel played a trick during Easter matins that led the priest and his maid to tear the hair of their farmers and go to war with them"; "How Eulenspiegel had his horse shod with gold shoes, for which the King of Denmark had to pay"; "How Eulenspiegel cheated the Jews at Frankfurt-on-the-Main out of a thousand guilders, by selling them his excrement as prophet's berries" (Oppenheimer translation).

As the last title suggests, the language of Bote's *Dyl Ulenspiegel* is anything but refined. Etymology links the protagonist's name with the so-called "Swabian greeting," insofar as *ulen* is a Low German verb meaning "to clean" and *spiegel* a North German expression for the human posterior. Ulenspiegel more than lives up to the anal associations of his name, exhibiting a veritable obsession with the fecal realm. Again, a sample of episode titles will say more than any summary description could: "How Eulenspiegel hired himself out to a furrier and shitted in his workroom for him, because one stink is supposed to drive out another"; "How Eulenspiegel shitted in the baths at Hanover, believing that the place was a House of Cleansing"; "How Eulenspiegel, in Bremen, basted his roast from his behind, so nobody wanted to eat it." Although defecation is a favorite theme of the book, other bodily functions also serve to demonstrate Eulenspiegel's wiliness, e.g., "How Eulenspiegel ate the white jam by himself, by letting a lump fall into it, out of his nose."

While its appeal may seem questionable to a late twentieth-century reader, Bote's *Dyl Ulenspiegel* was hugely popular in its day. It was widely printed, read, translated, and imitated; it has been estimated that some 30,000 copies appeared in the sixteenth century alone, making it one of the biggest fiction bestsellers of the time.[11] The influence of the title figure is such that echoes have been discerned in a number of twentieth-century literary protagonists, among them Thomas Mann's Felix Krull, Jaroslav Hasek's Good Soldier Svejk, the heroes of Karl Valentin's plays, and Oscar Matzerath in Günter Grass's *The Tin Drum,* as well as in the American boxer Cassius Clay.[12]

To this list must of course be added the Till Eulenspiegel of Christa and Gerhard Wolf. To answer the questions of what they do with the folktale written more than 450 years earlier and of how it is of use to them, it will be helpful to make some comparisons. One of the most obvious differences between Bote's book and the Wolfs' *Till Eulenspiegel* is that in the latter the setting is moved ahead two centuries, from the 1300s to the early sixteenth century, the era of Martin Luther, Charles V, Erasmus, Paracelsus—the last three of whom are mentioned in the Wolfs' text—and the eve of the German Peasant Wars (1524–1526). Like Bote's *Dyl,* the Wolfs' film narrative consists of episodes, although some 30 fewer than in the original. Only about 30 of the episodes in Bote's version appear in some form in the Wolfs' film narration, so that it is not correct to speak of a "reworking" of Bote's text; as Dieter Meyer and Wilfried Wulff express it, it is more accurate to regard the Wolfs' *Till Eulenspiegel* as the "result of a critical confrontation" with the sixteenth-century material.[13]

Stylistically, the Wolfs' language is highly realistic but far more uniform than Bote's sixteenth-century Saxon idiom, and for the most part their vocabulary is much more refined. But their film story is generically eclectic, weaving poems and songs into the prose narrative. Some of the earthy flavor of the folktale survives, for example in Eulenspiegel's practice of dousing a fire by urinating on it; in a scene in which he kills his horse, cuts open its belly, and stands inside it for protection; and in occasional scatological references, notably the episode in which Till deposits a pile of his excrement beneath a hat under which an aristocratic guest of the decadent nobleman Kunz, for whom Till works as a servant, has been expecting to find the first violet of spring as a gift.

The Wolfs' tale is related by a narrator who occasionally speaks in the first-person plural and comments on the times, as if to promote a certain camaraderie with the audience. Yet in general the story tells itself, so to speak, in a highly unmediated, dramatic fashion, as befits a film narrative. Dialogues are often included, in the manner of a play. Very short sentences, used frequently both to set the scene and convey the action, heighten the dramatic effect. The beginning of Episode 25 can serve to illustrate the style, structure, and tone of the Wolfs' *Till Eulenspiegel:*

An inn on the street. It is fairly empty. The sly-looking innkeeper attends
to his guests. Till showily seats himself at the "good table." The inn-
keeper is afraid to budge.
Till: "Can I eat well here—within my means?"
The innkeeper: "Of course, sir. You'll have everything you desire."
Till: "Then begin."
A maid brings wine. Till pinches her in the rear end, the way gentle-
men do these things.
He eats. The various courses are brought, soup, fish, poultry.
He eats.
The innkeeper, bathed in sweat, runs back and forth. Till keeps giving
commands: "More meat—within my means! A better wine—within my
means!"
Finally he has had enough. It's time to pay. Till sends three thin coins
dancing across the wooden table.
The innkeeper freezes: "You're joking, sir?"
Till stands up for himself: "Joking? Didn't you promise faithfully that
I could eat within my means? These are my means, I have no more. Do
you want to make a liar out of yourself?"[14]

As this passage demonstrates, the Wolfs' Till Eulenspiegel, like his
sixteenth-century predecessor, lives by his wits, above all by his skills as
a deceiver. Although he is merely a "little peasant" who often wears
fool's clothing or a fool's cap and is referred to as a "traveling fool," he is
clever at doing tricks, performing magic, making fun of others, recog-
nizing the weaknesses of those less perceptive than himself and exploit-
ing them to his advantage. Moreover, in contrast to Bote's Dyl, who
appears to be wholly lacking in sexual experience, Wolfs' Till Eulenspiegel has a way with women and often succeeds in winning over the
lovers of other men.

Till's outsider status, high degree of sensitivity, and unusual powers
of perception link him to Christa T., although the milieu in which he
lives is obviously quite different. Encountering the obstreperous and
tyrannical Kunz in his castle, a man whom most others fear and avoid,
Till diagnoses him as a lonely, unhappy man. Similarly, Till uses cunning
to figure out that Kunz is the father of his kitchen maid's bastard. Rec-
ognizing that Till has wholly seen through him, Kunz hires him as a
kind of all-purpose servant, a position that allows Till to demonstrate
his role-playing talents to their fullest. Till retains his powers of deception and trickery to the last. He saves himself near the end of his life by
feigning insanity, and, in an episode adapted from the sixteenth-century

text, he promises the people around his deathbed that all his earthly possessions are contained in a box that is to be buried with him and later exhumed; its contents are to be divided three ways, between the baron, the church, and themselves. When the box is dug up after his death, however, it is found to contain nothing but stones—a discovery that starts a fight between the baron, the cleric, and the peasants, each accusing the others of theft.

These illustrations of Till's talents as a trickster point as well toward the objects of satire in the Wolfs' *Till Eulenspiegel.* As in the original *Dyl Ulenspiegel,* the nobility and the clergy provide abundant joke material, but in the later work the emphasis is less on the foibles of these groups as types than on the extent to which they function as agents of power, oppressing those of a lower social status. The Wolfs' text is divided into two main parts, the first of which is entitled, significantly, "The Cunning of the Weak."

This difference reflects the fact that the Wolfs historicize and politicize the Eulenspiegel legend. Their satire of the church, for example, serves to unmask authority figures. In the mystery play with which the Wolfs' *Till Eulenspiegel* begins, the actor playing God the Father falls asleep out of boredom and is later heard to utter, "The devil take me" (*TE,* 6). Similarly, although Till witnesses a cripple regain the use of his legs after he kisses the toenails of a statue of Mary in the chapel, Till receives no answer to his repeated prayers to the same statue, because he has forgotten to kiss its feet. The questioning of religion implicit in the work's mockery of the elaborate trappings, rites, signs, and relics that are so important a part of the Catholic religion reaches its culmination in the dying Till's challenge to the priest: "Where is your God?" (*TE,* 204). But perhaps the work's most all-encompassing criticism of the church is summarized by a comment the narrator makes about some monks herding livestock into a pen: "The great belly of the church swallows everything" (*TE,* 17).

As this last observation in particular suggests, the Wolfs' critique of the church in *Till Eulenspiegel* can also be read as an attack on the East German socialist system; purporting to promote class equality, the system is in fact based on government hierarchies in which top-ranking functionaries, who have authority without always possessing the competence to justify it, enjoy privileges and material benefits denied to the population at large. Interpreted in this way, the Wolfs' *Till Eulenspiegel* is far removed from the doctrine of socialist realism, which as we have seen is intended to support and further the socialist state.

A comparable critique can be read in the Wolfs' depiction of the nobility in *Till Eulenspiegel*. The nobleman Kunz is frequently taken in by Till's tricks, such as when Till serves him a deep-fried cow patty that he consumes with relish. Emperor Charles V, whose court jester Till becomes, is portrayed as sickly, spoiled, and melancholic, reminiscent of a fairy-tale monarch in his habit of rewarding those who make him laugh. But the nobility and royalty in *Till Eulenspiegel* demonstrate worse traits than gullibility and weakness. Their gratuitous cruelty is most graphically manifested in Episode 43, in which a local prince and a group of his courtiers and hunters attack for no reason the members of a peaceful religious sect whom Till has befriended, abusing one of their women, throwing her baby down a well, and killing or chasing off the others. Till's attempts to divert the attackers by assuming his fool's garb and pretending to fly are of no avail against the prince, a "shrewd, cold person . . . to whom nothing is holy . . . for whom the frenzy of blood is the only thing that can drive off his boredom" (*TE*, 67, 69). Described at the conclusion of this episode as "powerless" (*TE*, 69) and weeping, Till emerges as a protagonist who differs sharply from the positive, active hero of socialist realism. While the Wolfs' Till Eulenspiegel can be seen to represent the plebeian class whose cause socialism supports in theory, his weakness and ineffectualness here suggest that they feel much remains to be done to translate this theory into practice.

Yet if the Wolfs find fault with the letter of socialism as it is practiced in the GDR, the fact that they nonetheless support its spirit is evident in the text, beginning with the epigraphs to the two major parts of the book: "In order for existing social conditions to be tampered with, their haloes had to be removed" (Friedrich Engels, *The Peasant War in Germany, TE*, 5); "One has to teach the people to be shocked at themselves in order to give them courage" (Karl Marx, *Contribution to the Critique of Hegel's Philosophy of Right, TE*, 5); "One must force these fossilized conditions to dance by singing them their own melody!" (Karl Marx, *Contribution to the Critique of Hegel's Philosophy of Right, TE*, 95).

The authors' choice of precisely these epigraphs is deliberate and judicious, for the statements can be seen to illuminate the need for social reform at three points in history: the German Peasant Wars of 1524–1526, in essence an early middle-class revolution in which peasants revolted against nobles in an effort to better their living and working conditions; the mid-nineteenth century, when Marx and Engels wrote in the hope of spurring the revolutionary development of communism; and the 1970s in the GDR, embodying a station farther down the road toward communism as envisioned by Marx and Engels but, in the Wolfs' view, still in need of improvement. Parallels can be seen between Till Eulenspiegel, actual sixteenth-century German peasants, and German workers of both the nineteenth and late twentieth centuries; the class system has produced difficulties for all of them, insofar as remnants of hierarchy still exist in East Germany, and radical means are often necessary for survival.

Till Eulenspiegel's role as a socialist before his time is evident in his exhortation to the young Charles V when the two first meet: "We have all been brothers since Adam's time. . . . It's just that the inheritance was distributed unequally. If you and I strip naked and exchange clothes, you'll see that all people are equal. Inequality comes from poverty and wealth alone" (*TE,* 143). Till's demand for equality literally goes with him to the grave—it appears on his tombstone. But the non-ideological, humanistic nature of his socialist philosophy, reflecting that of the Wolfs, is expressed in his deathbed wish: "Why shouldn't we be able to make human beings out of people?" (*TE,* 205).

"Kleiner Ausflug nach H."

Christa Wolf's writing career took yet another turn in 1974, which saw the publication of a collection of stories entitled *Unter den Linden: Drei unwahrscheinliche Geschichten* (Unter den Linden: Three Improbable Stories). In these stories a new element makes its appearance in her work, one that many critics viewed as wholly inappropriate to the doctrine of socialist realism: the fantastic. Since the typology devised by Tzvetan Todorov in his 1970 study of the subject, the fantastic in literature has come to be associated with uncertainty or hesitation about apparently supernatural occurrences. As opposed to the "uncanny," where seemingly supernatural events are eventually explained by scientific or natural laws (e.g., the banging window shutter turns out to have been caused by the wind), and to the "marvelous," in which the supernatural is simply accepted as supernatural (e.g., one believes that the ghost of a relative is haunting a house), in the fantastic mode it is impossible to determine which is the case; one "hesitates" between certainty and uncertainty about the supernatural status of the occurrence.[15]

The title story of the collection, "Unter den Linden," is a virtual dream narrative whose portrayal of the famous boulevard blurs the boundary between wakeful description and dreamlike envisioning; the second, "Neue Lebensansichten eines Katers," whose narrator and main character is a cat, is a satiric science-fiction response to E.T.A. Hoffmann's similarly titled novel. These stories will be discussed in chapter 5. The third story, "Selbstversuch: Traktat zu einem Protokoll," a futuristic second-person narrative in which a woman scientist who has undergone a sex-change experiment explains to the professor who conceived it and with whom she had been in love why she broke off the experiment before her transformation to a man was complete, will be treated in chapter 6.

"Kleiner Ausflug nach H." ("A Little Outing to H."), which was originally intended for inclusion in *Unter den Linden* but was not published until 1980, contains dreamlike elements but can nonetheless be read as a critique of the cultural politics of the GDR through its satire of East German literary doctrines, functionaries, and censors. The satire begins as a first-person narrator is driven by a friend to the town of Heldenstadt (Hero Town), called H. for short, and learns that their little excursion is taking place despite the efforts of the Society for Border-Crossing Tourist Traffic. Similarly, the narrator learns of the existence in Hero Town of a Committee for the Acknowledgment of New People and a Committee for Making the Slang used in Hero Town More Scientific. The satire continues as the narrator hears the so-called First Chairman give the same speech that he has already heard the Chairman's deputy give on the way into town; furthermore, the narrator is astonished to learn later in the same day that the First Chairman has to be replaced, according to instructions delivered by the same functionary who had defended the Chairman only the day before.

In the course of his excursion the narrator encounters the "Great Man"—that "larger-than-life stone figure standing on an ocher-colored pedestal in Great Man Square in the New People District of Hero Town" (*GE*, 135)—surely not an insignificant detail to a GDR readership familiar with statues of Marx and Engels throughout the country and with the general East German practice of venerating communist thinkers and political leaders. And the narrator's observation that the inhabitants not only of Hero Town but of the entire country he is visiting are particularly adept at controlling their faces has more meaning than ever now that the GDR no longer exists and the State Security Service (Stasi), or Secret Police, has been cracked open to reveal a massive, wide-ranging bureaucracy in which, it is estimated, one in every 50 citizens was involved, either as an employee or as an informant. Christa Wolf, having herself collaborated with the Stasi between 1959 and 1962, reflects in this comment of the narrator her awareness of the extent to which the GDR was a society of spies in which it was difficult ever to feel completely certain that one's actions or words were not being observed. But the primary object of satirical critique in "Kleiner Ausflug nach H." is an aesthetic one. The narrator is told that some of inhabitants of Hero Town are precisely that—literary (or film or television) heroes, while others—those who wear an orange badge with a black "P" for "person"—are people; the fictional figures act out the plots of the works in which they were created, and their dress and the homes in which they live are true to the settings and periods of the works, not of the GDR in the 1970s. In a fashion reminiscent of Lewis Carroll's *Alice in Wonderland,* the residents of Hero Town can be seen to exist on two fictional levels: all exist on the fictional level created by Christa Wolf, and some also exist on the metafictional level of the works of literature, television, and film for which they were created, *within* the fictional framework of the story. Little wonder that the narrator, thinking about the so-called Sector R (for "Reality") outside, muses to himself how relative words like "inside" and "outside" are.

Numerous details in "Kleiner Ausflug nach H." suggest that Wolf's aim is not to mock the desire of art to capture life but that her specific target is socialist realism. A student of German literature, Rüdiger Milbe, informs the narrator that he has chosen Hero Town for his internship since it is an especially popular testing ground for literary scholars—"because of its trueness-to-life" (*GE,* 131). To invoke this criterion of socialist realism in a metafictional text like this one can only produce amusement. Other satirical references include the "Action Joy of Life," a program that a sociologist who appeared in an artistic newspaper has been commissioned to carry out by encouraging the citizens of his district to greet each other with the phrase "Joy of Life!" (GE, 136); the satiric barb of this allusion is two-sided, since it also calls forth associations to the language of national socialism.

But probably the most explicit lampoon of the socialist realist aesthetic is found in the story's manipulation of the term "positive hero," which as we have seen is one of the most crucial requirements of a socialist realist work. In Rüdiger's equation of the term "positive hero" with the term "new person" (*neuer Mensch*), which most educated German readers would recognize as a catchword of German expressionism, Wolf brings together two contradictory aesthetic programs, thus implicitly undermining both. Moreover, details such as a bar in Hero Town "for positive heroes with small human flaws" (*GE,* 140) and characters the

narrator encounters who have been removed from literary works
because of their psychological instability further appear to play with
socialist realism's advocacy of a positive hero who embodies the utopian
future of socialism.

Complementing the satire of socialist realism in "Kleiner Ausflug
nach H." is the mockery of the propagandistic picture of the West created and disseminated by the East German government. Hero Town
contains a district of poor Westerners, associated with "an odor of foreign gasoline and a certain luxury . . . for the most part created by writers of crime novels who make a lot of money and find their criminals
and crooks beyond the borders of their country" (GE, 144). Echoing the
critical rhetoric of the actual GDR government, these fictional Westerners are accustomed to having "the two big Cs of the corrupt Western
system—consumption and comfort" (GE, 144), and they develop a
snobbish taste for Eastern paraphernalia such as red flags, party badges,
and symbols of other progressive organizations. As a prize-winning
author with extensive privileges, including travel to the Federal Republic of Germany as well as numerous other countries in the West, Wolf
has enough empirical evidence to recognize that East Germans' stereotypes about their brother country to the west are only partially true, and
she uses humor as a corrective for her readers.

The fanciful nature of "Kleiner Ausflug nach H." is strengthened by a
number of dreamlike elements. Before traveling to H. the narrator's
friend refuses to divulge their destination or even the direction in which
they will be going. Following their excursion the narrator, claiming that
he might have fallen asleep in the car, has no recollection of their return
trip or of their arrival, and only wakes up the next morning in the hotel
room where he had been before the trip. When he speaks to the friend
about it, the friend has no memory of an excursion.

Was the excursion to H., then, only a dream? Did it "happen"? In a
metafictional realm like the one in which this story operates, it is difficult to talk about truth and fiction. Even though the validity of the
excursion within the text is thrown into question, the trip nonetheless
takes place on the imaginative level; the reader absorbs it and its critique of GDR institutions. By the late 1970s, Christa Wolf's identity as
a committed East German writer who wants to see her country on the
path to the right kind of socialism is firm. From such a commitment
there was no turning back.

Chapter Four
Coming to Terms with Fascism

Dealing with the Fascist Past
in East and West Germany

As has become especially evident since the fall of the Berlin Wall in 1989, the German Democratic Republic failed to confront sufficiently its complicity in the crimes committed by Germany during the Third Reich. In the years immediately following the war, fascism was a taboo topic in both East and West Germany; the horrors were simply too close and too immediate to contemplate. Eventually the GDR, viewing itself as the heir of the proletarian and revolutionary potential offered by the Weimar Republic and the antifascist resistance, came to regard fascism as a chapter that had been closed by the founding of a socialist state; socialism was virtually equated with antifascism. In general East Germans tended to transfer responsibility for coming to terms with the German fascist past onto the Federal Republic, as if the years from 1933 to 1945 could thereby be erased from the East German calendar. From the late 1950s on, West German authors did indeed begin the difficult business of what came to be known as *Vergangenheitsbewältigung,* or "coming to terms with the past" (literally, "conquering the past"). Paul Celan's "Todesfuge" (1952; "Death Fugue") and other poems; Günter Grass's *Die Blechtrommel* (1959; *The Tin Drum*) and *Katz und Maus* (1961; *Cat and Mouse*); Heinrich Böll's *Billard um halbzehn* (1959; *Billiards at Half-Past Nine*) and other novels and stories; Rolf Hochhuth's *Der Stellvertreter* (1963; *The Deputy*); and Peter Weiss's *Die Ermittlung* (1965; *The Investigation*) represent some of the most important attempts to uncover and examine the psychological, moral, emotional, and physical wounds inflicted by the Third Reich.

Since the resistance to fascism—in effect, the denial of it—was built into the ideology on which the GDR was founded, the rhetoric of this resistance was more widespread there than in the Federal Republic. The language of fascist resistance was disseminated by East German history textbooks used in schools as well as by film and literature. Sonja Hilzinger distinguishes two phases in East German literature's treatment of fascism:

1. The glorification of antifascist resistance, especially on the part of communists.
2. A later phase portraying a kind of "denazification": former Nazis or Nazi sympathizers are often transformed into committed socialists.[1]

For Christa Wolf, neither the West German attitude that the fascist past could be "conquered" or atoned for by writing about it nor the East German inclination to deny the effects of fascism by resisting it or whitewashing it away was sufficient. For her, the impact of the Third Reich on those who lived through it was all-pervasive and long-lasting, enduring far beyond the termination of Hitler's regime. As she demonstrates in the story "Blickwechsel" (1970; "Exchanging Glances") and especially the novel *Kindheitsmuster* (1976; *Patterns of Childhood*), for members of her generation of Germans, the years between 1933 and 1945 were the formative influence on their lives and made them what they are today. Wolf's willingness to acknowledge her participation in this most troubling chapter of German history sets her apart from the majority of her fellow writers in the GDR.

The Importance of Anna Seghers for Wolf

A crucial model and mentor for Wolf in confronting Germany's fascist past is Anna Seghers. Born Netty Reiling into a well-to-do Jewish family in Mainz in 1900, Seghers joined the communist party in 1928, motivated by a fervent belief in the Soviet Union; as Wolf quotes her avowing at the time of the Russian Revolution, "my whole disposition was communist."[2] Forced to leave Germany in 1933, Seghers lived first in France, then she emigrated to Mexico. She returned after the war but, like Bertolt Brecht, settled not in West but in East Germany, where she became one of the state's most respected voices in cultural affairs. She served as president of the Writers' Union from 1952 to 1978 and died in 1983.

In the 1960s and early 1970s Wolf devoted several essays to Seghers, whose works she knows intimately. Her commitment to the older writer endured into the 1980s and 1990s, when she edited a collection of Seghers' stories and wrote an afterword to it (1983) and later wrote a brief personal introduction to an illustrated biography of Seghers, published by Aufbau Verlag in 1994. It is the earlier essays with which we are more concerned here. In them Wolf expresses her admiration for many facets of Seghers' style, among them her moderation and control and her realism. Wolf writes that Seghers, remarking the absence of a great tradition of the realist novel in German, schooled herself in the French and Russian realists, in particular Balzac, Tolstoy, and Dostoyevsky.[3] Above all, Wolf praises what she calls Seghers' "faith in the terrestrial"—which Wolf defines in her essay "Glauben an Irdisches" ("Faith in the Terrestrial") as "earthly reason, thinking, feeling, understanding, and acting reason. . . . the courage for revolutionary deeds, the boldness for seemingly hopeless endeavors that, even if many of them fail, are in their totality the only assurance of the survival of the terrestrial."[4]

Of most relevance to Wolf's works about fascism is Seghers' novel *Das siebte Kreuz* (1942; *The Seventh Cross*), to which Wolf devoted an entire essay as well as portions of others. Seghers' best-known novel, written while the author was in exile in France, portrays seven escaped inmates of a concentration camp near Mainz. Only one reaches the Dutch border and thus freedom. The title refers to the fact that the commander of the camp has crosses nailed to seven trees in the expectation that each prisoner will be caught and bound to a cross; the empty cross reserved for the only one of the seven prisoners to survive hence becomes a powerful symbol of resistance. Wolf's summary of the novel's plot is pithy: "The simplest thing offers itself: a communist, escaped from the concentration camp, runs for his life and forces everyone with whom he comes into contact to show what he is worth" ("GI," 121).

It goes without saying that *Das siebte Kreuz,* which dared to treat the phenomenon of fascism while Hitler was still in power in order to warn his victims, could not appear in print in the country whose political system it attacks; it was published in English in 1942 by an American press and in German at the same time in Mexico. Brought out in East Germany after the war, it can in retrospect be seen to belong to the first phase in the East German literary treatment of fascism, mentioned above—the glorification of antifascist resistance, especially on the part of communists—although the initial part of this phase preceded the existence of East Germany. The novel was quickly adopted by East German schools, where Wolf encountered it in 1948. She finds it "breathtaking," admires its "nearly uncanny sureness in characterizing people and their transformation beneath the fascist dictatorship, their deformation or self-preservation" ("SK," 192, 184). In her view this book is made of a "material [that is] lasting and indestructible like little else in the world. It is called justice" ("SK," 193).

In other words, Anna Seghers achieves what Wolf, too, would like to achieve, but what she is not yet quite ready to undertake in 1963, the year this essay is published. Wolf's identification with Seghers, implicit in many passages of her essays on the older writer, is made explicit in her essay of 1974: "There are moments when my viewpoint is transformed through hers and—insofar as it is possible to say this—even into hers" ("FV," 154). In "Glauben an Irdisches," which appeared in 1968, Wolf attributes two major objectives to Seghers that she herself was to pursue during the subsequent decade: to defeat fascism in people's minds after it had been defeated militarily, and to demonstrate the inextricable connections between the writer's personal life and the "stormy, often cruel, shocking, life of the times, which sometimes carries the writer along with it" ("GI," 132, 141). As we will see, these are two of the major goals of Wolf's *Kindheitsmuster.*

"Blickwechsel"

Both the story "Blickwechsel" and the long narrative work *Kindheitsmuster* exemplify an insight Wolf voices in her seminal essay "Lesen und Schreiben" (1968; "Reading and Writing"): "Since the labor of writing has never been completely abandoned, even in the most difficult of times, it seems that stark, sheer life—undescribed, untransmitted, uninterpreted, and unmediated—cannot so easily come to terms with itself." Specifically, what we need is prose: "[Prose] would only be truly saved if we could figure out that it is important for us—possibly a matter of life and death—to follow where it can lead us."[5] Prose is for Wolf, both as reader and writer of it, the crucial means to make sense of her life and thereby understand herself. Nowhere is this truer than with regard to her fascist past, the most sensitive and emotionally laden subject she had dealt with hitherto.

If the lengthy and complex *Kindheitsmuster* represents Wolf's sustained grapple with her past in fascist Germany, "Blickwechsel" can be said to offer a brief preview of what is to come. The story treats a moment that occurs late in the novel and late in the war, the spring of 1945, when the Allies are liberating Germany from Hitler's rule. The story is in most respects autobiographical, as is the novel: the 16-year-old first-person narrator is fleeing west to escape the advancing Russians with her family, who owns a grocery store. Although the story is understandably more concentrated and elliptical than the novel, which expounds more fully on characters and incidents, many of the characters who appear in *Kindheitsmuster* have their debut in "Blickwechsel," such as the narrator's mother and younger brother; the imperious landowners Herr und Frau Volk (altered to "Folk" in *Kindheitsmuster*); and the Grunds, a farming family. The multitude of aunts and uncles and the two pairs of grandparents who are featured in the novel are condensed in the story into a single aunt, uncle, grandmother, and grandfather.

Similarly, "Blickwechsel" contains a number of striking details that recur in *Kindheitsmuster,* for example the bombers passing overhead on their way to Berlin; the toothless grandfather who cuts tiny notches into crusts of bread so that he can chew them; the frozen baby that the narrator, not knowing that it is dead, passes on to its refugee mother, who becomes hysterical; and the narrator's negative reactions to the American occupying forces. The two most important scenes that occur in both story and novel are the death of the foreman Wilhelm Grund and the narrator's encounter with a group of concentration camp inmates. The death of Grund, a civilian who is shot in the belly by strafe fire and dies virtually before the eyes of his horrified wife and four children, is echoed shortly thereafter in the death of the narrator's family's ox, which has to be shot after it is wounded by gunfire from Allied planes.

These scenes are significant for the psychological development of the young narrator. The shooting of Grund makes her aware of the arbitrariness of death—and of the fragility of life—since it was only by chance that her family's wagon was not in the line of fire. The sight of both the dying ox and the inmates from the concentration camp fills the narrator with guilt. The language describing both situations is illuminating with regard to the story's title. As the narrator forces herself to look at the ox about to be shot, she speculates, "That couldn't be an accusation I saw in its gaze, so why did I feel guilty?"[6] In like manner, she observes about the inmates, "Then we saw the concentration camp inmates. . . . These people, who had been declared animals and who were now coming slowly toward us to take their revenge—we had abandoned them. Now these people in rags would put on our clothes, would stick their bloody feet into our shoes; now the starving would grab away the butter and flour and sausage that we had just managed to find. And with horror I realized: this is justice, and for a fraction of a second I knew that we were guilty. I forgot it again. . . . They silently looked down at us. I couldn't stand to look at them" (*GE,* 16).

In both these highly candid revelations, physical sight leads to higher insight on the part of the young narrator. Both shades of meaning are captured by the story's richly evocative title, which is a play on words; "Blickwechsel" means literally, "exchange of glances" and metaphorically, "change of perspective." Although the narrator can force herself to stare at the wounded ox despite the guilt it inspires, the guilt produced in her by the gaze of the emaciated, exhausted concentration camp inmates is so great that she feels compelled to evade both seeing them and being seen by them. This distinction serves to emphasize the plight of the inmates: although those in power have pronounced them animals in order to justify their extermination, it is precisely the fact that they are not animals but human beings—a contrast underlined by the parallel incident with the wounded ox—that renders the guilt of those who stood silently by all the greater. In the case of the narrator, this guilt is compounded at the end of the story when, in an incident that is enlarged and elaborated in the novel, a demoralized and baffled concentration camp inmate asks her and her family, "Where in the world have you been all these years?" (*GE,* 19).

The other meaning of the story's title, "change of perspective," is exemplified in a number of ways in the text, suggesting that one's perspective on the events narrated is as important as the events themselves— a belief that we have seen to be central to Wolf's oeuvre. Within the story we find first of all a change of perspective in the narrator herself, a change that accompanies maturity. Contemplating the span of time between the summer of 1939 and the present moment, she notes, "In those six years I had stopped being a child" (*GE,* 15)—a transformation that has been brought about by much more than the mere passage of time.

The narrator's perspective on her fellow Germans has also been altered by the events of the war. In the face of meaningless bloodshed like the death of Wilhelm Grund, it becomes less and less clear which side is "right" and which "wrong"; describing the aftermath of Grund's death, the narrator tells us, "I didn't ask who my mother meant when she embraced Frau Grund and said loudly, 'Damn them. These damned criminals' " (*GE,* 12). A similar change of perspective, bringing sadness along with its wisdom, is embodied in the narrator's realization that the Germans, defeated, now occupy a subordinate position and that the victorious Americans are in charge. This insight is perhaps most memorably portrayed in the story's final scene, set on 5 May 1945—an American soldier with a squealing German girl on each arm. Despite all the horrors she has witnessed in the course of the story, it is only this sight that brings the narrator to tears, in a moment that seems in its private capitulation to foreshadow microcosmically the national surrender that is just days away.

In light of the story's attention to the changes of perspective in the narrator as a character, it is interesting by contrast to note the references to the constancy of the narrator's perspective as a narrator. The narrator claims that she can see the narrated events as clearly now as in the past: "All these years this moment [of liberation] has been needle-sharp before my eyes, it is tucked away in my memory as a finished piece, and if there have been reasons not to touch it until now, then twenty-five years must have destroyed, or at least faded, these reasons" (*GE,* 10). The narrator moreover reveals that the sharp-sighted perspective she holds today was gained back then; with regard to the period of her family's flight to the west she tells us, "It's impossible to see oneself when one is lost in oneself, but I saw all of us just as I see us today, as if someone had taken me out of my shell and set me down next to it, commanding, 'Look!' " (*GE,* 7–8).

This cogency of narrative perspective is merely one of the features that distinguish "Blickwechsel" from *Kindheitsmuster.* Whereas the story is told by an "I," a pronoun designating unified, homogeneous narrating and narrated selves that are continuous with each other, the novel, reflecting the loss of this continuity, employs a combination of second- and third-person narrative voices. Similarly, while "Blickwechsel" is narrated in a linear manner, the novel takes place on three temporal levels at once. The novel, in other words, loosens its ties to the realistic technique employed in "Blickwechsel," which is intimated in an observation made by the story's narrator as her family sets off on its flight before the advancing Russian army: "[My mother] hitches herself to the front of the cart, my brother and I push from behind, the sky provides uncanny fireworks in accompaniment, and once again I hear the subtle noise with which the conventional train *Reality* jumps out of its tracks and races wildly right into the most unbelievable unreality, which makes me shake with laughter whose impropriety I am keenly aware of" (*GE,* 6). Whereas the real may at times seem unreal in "Blickwechsel," it is throughout narrated in a realistic fashion. By the time she writes *Kindheitsmuster,* Wolf has abandoned this mode of narration.

Kindheitsmuster

Reading both "Blickwechsel" and *Kindheitsmuster* autobiographically, as the facts invite us to do, we recognize that despite the heavy-hearted presentiment of the story's narrator on leaving her hometown in 1945, she does in fact see it again. As we learn in the course of the novel, *Kindheitsmuster* was inspired by a trip its narrator took in July 1971 to her hometown, now in Poland and called G., formerly in Germany and known as L.—just as Wolf grew up in Landsberg an der Warthe, Germany, which became the Polish Gorzów Wielkopolski after the war. Although the trip to the place where she grew up, undertaken with the narrator's husband H., her younger brother Lutz, and her 14-year-old daughter Lenka, occupies no more than 46 hours, it provokes powerful emotional reactions in the narrator and unleashes memories that must be dealt with. For a year she searches for the proper beginning for the novel; after 36 false starts she achieves it.[7]

As mentioned above, the novel takes place on three time levels. Details in the text make it possible to specify these levels precisely:

1. The period spanned by the book's composition—from 3 November 1972 to 2 May 1975.
2. The days covered by the trip to Poland, 10–11 July 1971.
3. The period from roughly 1932 to 1947.

As was also indicated earlier, however, until the end of the novel the narrator does not speak as "I" but splits herself into a "you," whom she addresses as her adult self, and a "she," designated "Nelly Jordan," the name she ascribes to her childhood self. This technique, which in terms of cultural history may be seen as typical of the postmodernist conception of the self as fragmented and constructed, has specific significance for the narrator (and for Wolf). It reflects her awareness that the person she is today, although indebted to her past selves, is not identical with them.

This concern with what might be called the genealogy of the adult self is everywhere evident in *Kindheitsmuster.* The question "How have we become the way we are today?," which constitutes both the title and the last sentence of chapter 9, can be regarded as the point of departure of the novel. Phrasing it another way, the narrator asks, "Could it be true that the basic character of a human being is formed by the fifth year of his life?"[8] The narrator's sense of the importance of childhood in shaping character and of the effects of youthful experiences on adulthood is reflected in her conception of a continuity between the past and our remembrance of the past in the present. The book opens with the lines, "The past is not dead; it is not even past" (*KM,* 9); shortly afterward the narrator claims, "The present intrudes upon remembrance, and today is already the last day of the past" (*KM,* 9). This sense of past and present as intermingled is evident also in the narrator's hope that she can learn about her daughter Lenka by mentally "revisiting" Nelly.

With respect to *Kindheitsmuster* one could also say that the past intrudes upon the remembrance of the more distant past, as is evident for example in the narrator's present recollection of a moment in the city park in her hometown during the trip a year and a half earlier in which she had remembered an even earlier scene in the same park from Nelly's childhood. This phenomenon of "metamemory"—the memory of a memory—is especially illustrative of an image mentioned in the novel that could serve as an apt metaphor for the workings of memory, the tertiary, or a pre-human era of the geological past whose tracks and traces can be read in order to learn about forms of life that no longer exist. As with the layers of earth, fossils, and artifacts uncovered by a geological dig, each level of memory serves to shed light both on those that have preceded it and on those that follow it.

But the importance of Wolf's awareness of the interworkings of past and present is not limited to the personal realm. The narrator's mention of "history's fatal tendency to repeat itself, a phenomenon for which we must prepare ourselves" (*KM,* 159) points to the larger significance of what can be called the false dichotomy between past and present. While her story focuses on the Third Reich, the narrator makes frequent reference to political events from the years in which she is writing, such as the Vietnam War and the results of the coup in Chile—the murder of Allende and many of his followers and the seizure of power by Pinochet. While these instances of genocide and dictatorship are not precisely parallel to those that characterized the Germany in which the narrator grew up, the similarities are clear.

The intricate interconnections between past and present and the importance of memory for the present are manifest also in the style of *Kindheitsmuster.* Our memories do not proceed logically but are free-floating and wide-ranging—we may think about what we had for breakfast this morning, which reminds us of something we ate as a child, which leads to another childhood memory, which triggers thoughts of a current friend, which reminds us of a piece of clothing we want to buy, which produces an erotic fantasy, and so forth. In like manner, the narrator's memories in the novel are neither logical nor chronological but jump around among the three time levels, creating an effect akin to a collage. An editorial comment made by the narrator is illuminating in this connection: "Ideally, the structures of experience should coincide with the structures of narration. The goal would be fantastic accuracy. But no technique exists that would allow an incredibly interwoven web, whose strands are plaited together according to the strictest laws, to be translated into linear language without doing it serious damage" (*KM*, 251–52). An earlier narratorial observation takes note of the novel's voluminous eclecticism: "Nearly everything belongs in here: it has come to that. The pull this work exerts keeps getting stronger" (*KM*, 90).

And yet *Kindheitsmuster* is not a stream-of-consciousness narrative, in which the author typically strives to convey an impression of random all-inclusiveness. Moreover, the fact that there are no transitions between memories from the three different levels in Wolf's narrative serves to reinforce the reader's sense of their influence on each other. Although the narrator skips around temporally on the "micro" level, moving for example from a memory of her trip to Poland to a vignette about Nelly's childhood to a political event from the 1970s, there is a loose chronological progression from the book's beginning to its end on the "macro" level in that the earlier chapters focus mainly on Nelly's earlier childhood, the middle ones on her middle years, and the last chapters on her later teenage years. There are also repetitions and continuities between the levels, as when Lenka is described as having played the same games Nelly did.

The extent to which the style of the book is not random but in fact (of necessity) carefully constructed can be microcosmically illustrated by analysis of a passage that reveals a kind of method behind the collage principle that governs much of the novel's structure. The passage occurs at the end of chapter 13:

> Can't write another line. It's evening. On television a choir of elderly black men sings: Oh when the saints go marchin' in . . .
> Music by Bach.
> The train wreck in Zagreb was caused by human error.
> In G. (formerly L.), a little town in Poland, you ate breakfast early on Sunday, July 11, 1971, around 9, in a milk bar near the marketplace.
> "I have written a good deal in order to lay the foundation for memory." Johann Wolfgang Goethe. (*KM*, 266–67)

Although the temporal point of departure for this passage is the narrator's present—the 1970s—it obviously contains images from other periods as well. From the present moment stem the televised images of black men singing an American classic and the accident in Zagreb; the music by Bach is perceived by the narrator in the present but acts as a temporal, cultural, and stylistic counterpoint to the song being performed on television, hence functioning in much the same way that the quotation from Goethe does vis-à-vis both the black music and the narrator's own writing. The train wreck, evoking an image of mass death, is implicitly connected to the theme of mass death associated with both the Third Reich and the Vietnam War, yet mention of the cause of the accident points up, by contrast, the fact that both these other events were the result not of human failure but of deliberate choice. The recording of a detail from the 1971 trip to Poland, one of the main sources of memories in the book, leads in turn to the citation touching on the relationship between writing and memory for a writer often mentioned, with admiration, in the novel.

Counterpoint and parallelism, juxtaposition of temporal levels, association—the features evident in this passage are typical of the means the narrator employs in piecing together her text. Association is especially frequent, though often implicit, as in a passage in which the narrator observes that because of the war Nelly never had the opportunity to be a real teenager and in addition wanted to look older than she was; without transition, the next paragraph relates that the narrator and H. come home and find a note from their daughter Lenka saying that she has once again failed to do her math, to clean her room, and to take a shower, since these things are simply not that important to her. Rather than making the contrast explicit, the narrator leaves it up to the reader, yet it is clear nonetheless, contributing to the novel's exploration of the relationship between childhood and adulthood, past and present.

The apparent distinction between past and present, then, is revealed in *Kindheitsmuster* to be a spurious one. A second dichotomy that the work undermines is that between novel and autobiography. On the one hand, Wolf makes no effort to disguise the many elements from her own life that are incorporated into the text, some of which have been mentioned. Like Wolf, Nelly is born in 1929 in a German town beginning with "L." that after the war becomes the Polish "G."; her parents, like Wolf's, own and operate a grocery store; Nelly attends school in L., as Wolf had done in Landsberg; near the end of the war Nelly's family escapes advancing Russian troops by fleeing west, as did Wolf's family; like Wolf, Nelly next works as a clerical assistant to the mayor of a small town and then comes down with tuberculosis. Both the narrator and

Wolf are writers who have intellectual husbands, two daughters, a brother three years younger, and so forth. Moreover, the autobiographical narrator reveals that she has done research to authenticate her facts. She has visited the State Library in (then) West Berlin to read newspapers printed in her hometown from the years she is depicting, and she has studied school textbooks from the same period to refresh her memory about the indoctrination she and her classmates received.

On the other hand, much in the text points to the difficulty or even impossibility of "telling" one's life story accurately. One of the central mechanisms involved in this process is of course memory, a faculty to which the narrator pays a good deal of attention. She comments on the unreliability of memory and speculates often on the nature and workings of it: "Memory. According to today's definition: 'The preservation of earlier experience and the ability to preserve it.' Not an organ, then, but rather an activity and the capacity for carrying it out, in a word. An unused memory gets lost, no longer exists, dissolves into nothing—an alarming thought" (*KM*, 15).

It is in part because of the unreliable and subjective nature of memory that postmodernist theory often places autobiography on the boundary between fact and fiction. Postmodernism also doubts the existence of a cohesive, continuous entity such as is designated by the pronoun "I." That Christa Wolf shares both kinds of skepticism is evident again and again in *Kindheitsmuster*. Her awareness of the power of imagination and thought over reality, with its capacity to turn supposed fact into fiction, is reflected for instance in the narrator's comment that "Could it be that the richness of childhood everyone feels results from the fact that we ceaselessly embellish this period by the excessive rethinking that we devote to it?" (*KM*, 30).

Wolf underlines the fictional quality of her narrative in a number of ways. Most obviously, the West German edition of the work bears the designation *Roman*—novel—as its subtitle, although the American translation does not retain this.[9] Furthermore, the author includes a disclaimer at the beginning of the work stating that all the characters are invented, that none is identical with an actual person living or dead, and that events described in the text do not correspond to actual occurrences. While it is not unusual to find such a disclaimer at the beginning of a novel, one does not expect it of autobiography. This disclaimer, like the device of giving her childhood self an invented name and self-consciously calling attention to it, represents Wolf's fictionalization of a period of her life from which she now feels alienated. The narrator's recounting the conversation with her husband in which they try out a series of titles for the book similarly heightens its novelistic status, as does the occasional use of capital letters for the names of cities and persons rather than providing them in full.

Other features in *Kindheitsmuster* typical of fiction include the device of the narrator, which this narrator justifies as follows: "But the retrieval of memories—which by the way differs markedly in people who have supposedly had the exact same experience—is probably not a function of biochemistry and does not seem to be available to all of us everywhere. If it were otherwise, that which many claim would be true: documents could not be surpassed and would make the narrator superfluous" (*KM,* 69). But this particular narrator frequently calls attention to her lack of omniscience, as in the *Kristallnacht* (Night of Broken Glass) scene on 9 November 1938, in which Nelly goes to view a burning synagogue in her town. The feigned ignorance expressed in phrases like "Somebody must have told Nelly the synagogue was burning," "Perhaps she did not yet know the word [ruin]," "One of the small houses must have had a dark gateway where Nelly could hide," "She probably leaned against the wall or against one of the wings of the gate," "She was probably wearing her dark blue sweatsuit" (*KM,* 150), serves to heighten the sense of alienation and distance the narrator feels from her participation, even as an observer, in the Third Reich and to increase the fictionality of the events narrated.

Finally, the novelistic character of *Kindheitsmuster* is further reinforced by its symbolism. To cite merely one example, in connection with the Jordan family's evacuation in 1945 the narrator claims that "Photos that one has looked at often and long do not burn easily" (*KM,* 29). The use of a metaphor to talk about the difficulty of letting go of the past—one of the dominant themes of the book—is typical of the work's figurative style and reflects its narrator's interest in "the power of the unreal, imagined, wished-for over the real things in life" (*KM,* 61).

The poles of the dichotomy spanned by *Kindheitsmuster* are well summed up in Wolf's description in the essay "Lesen und Schreiben" of the autobiographical narrator's method (her own) in the face of the impossibility of objectivity and the imperfect nature of memory: "He [the narrator] decides to tell the story, that is, to invent something faithful to the truth that is based on his own experience" ("LS," 27). The fact that I have been referring to the book as a novel and to the voice speaking it as its narrator suggests that I incline toward regarding the book as fiction. However, it seems most accurate to view it as a hybrid between autobiography and novel, as an autobiographical novel, with features and elements of both modes. *Kindheitsmuster* stands as an eloquent demonstration of the fact that autobiography is far from pure nonfiction, just as the novel as genre has always drawn its lifeblood from the experiential realm.

A third dichotomy undermined by *Kindheitsmuster* is that between private and public. The extent to which the two realms are interlinked in the narrative that focuses on Nelly's childhood between 1932 and 1947 reflects the fact that in a dictatorship there is no such thing as genuinely private life; the state has a hand in everything, whether seen or unseen. Reference is made, to be sure, to details of Nelly's personal development, such as her entrance into puberty, her sense of a lack of communication with her parents and her resulting feelings of lovelessness, her crushes on various teachers, her feelings of awkwardness and sadness as a teenager, tales of boys who are interested in her, questions of diet and clothes, and the like. Yet *Kindheitsmuster* is anything but the story of a girl's private growth into young womanhood. In keeping with her interest in how we have become what we are, the narrator depicts Nelly's development primarily insofar as it reflects the influence of the larger entities of family, school, and nation, which are themselves tightly intertwined with each other.

We learn, for example, about Nelly's commitment to the Hitler Youth, one of the principal organs for disseminating national socialist ideology to an impressionable and largely willing population. She not only enjoys the comradeship and diversion offered by the group meetings but becomes an accomplished athlete in the organization, attaining a position as one of the ten best on the team of the *Jungmädel* (a branch of the Hitler Youth for young girls). Paralleling her energetic participation in the Hitler Youth is Nelly's faith in the Führer himself. She is guided and inspired by his sayings, which she and the other Jungmädel are encouraged to repeat often; a particular favorite of hers is, "You must practice the virtues today that nations need if they want to become great. You must be loyal, you must be brave, and you must form a single, great, glorious comradeship with each other" (*KM,* 187). Motivated by these doctrines, while once serving on inspection duty at the Jungmädel camp, Nelly turns in a friend for habits of grooming and cleanliness that are less than ideal. Nelly's justification: she was just doing her duty, without favoritism.

Nelly's behavior reflects the influence of other elements of Third Reich ideology as well. The narrator recounts what could be called a racial primal scene that occurs in 1936 or 1937, when Nelly is only seven or eight years old. Witnessing the distressed state of one of her aunts because she is suspected of being half-Jewish, the young Nelly runs away and hides, exclaiming, "I don't want to be a Jew!" (*KM*, 133). Later, she writes a poem for an anti-Semitic teacher, Herr Warsinski, which includes the lines, "The German people were surrounded by enemies / In the great world conflagration, / But our brave German soldiers / Let no enemy into the country. / Through contemptuous treason by Jews / Peace was made with Germany" (*KM*, 123). Similarly, in Nelly's memory the image of a Jewish boy whom an acquaintance of her father tells of having persecuted in school gets mixed up with the disgusting sight of the "white snake" of a man who once exposed himself to her.

Much of the guilt Nelly appears to bear in her anti-Semitism is tantamount to the sin of being a bystander, a transgression that the 16-year-old Nelly also acknowledges in connection with her calm response to a report in 1945 that her father might be dead. But where did this "sin" originate? Writing about Nelly's actions on 9 November 1938 (the Night of Broken Glass), the narrator suggests that Nelly was forced as a child to turn compassion for the weak and inferior into hate and fear, that "she had long ago begun to deny her true feelings to herself" (*KM*, 150–51). As the novel demonstrates, the institutions of family, school, and nation all contribute to these processes of displacement, denial, and repression in Nelly. From her mother she learns control: "That's the thing every human being has to learn, or else he's not a human being. One must be able to control oneself!" (*KM*, 58). Revolt against this family is out of the question. In a very telling comment the narrator observes, "Sometime or other [in her first three years] [the reasonable child] learned that being obedient and being loved are one and the same thing" (*KM*, 20).

It goes without saying that school is a powerful influence on any young person, and during the Third Reich German schools were strictly monitored for ideological correctness. Herr Warsinski encourages the girls in his class to wash their upper bodies in ice-cold water, "as is fitting for a German girl" (*KM*, 97). This same teacher is full of fire and brimstone against the Jews and in favor of the Führer, exclaiming to the class, "Silence, please! Where do you think you are, in a Jew school? . . . Whoever disgraces me when we salute the flag is going to get it! Our Führer works day and night for us, and you can't even keep quiet for ten minutes?" (*KM*, 95). The occasion is the Führer's forty-seventh birthday, and the school is bending over backwards to honor him, offering not only a salute to the flag by all the pupils but a speech by the principal. Finally, the influence of the national socialist state, as embodied in so-called national virtues, is evident throughout the text, as for example in the frequent reference to the fact that "a German girl does not cry" (*KM,* 124).

Not only does Nelly's development reflect the influences on her of the institutions of family, school, and state; the family as depicted in *Kindheitsmuster* and exemplified in the Jordans can be seen as microcosmic of Germany during the Third Reich. The portrayal of this family is only conceivable against this historical backdrop. Again the dividing line between private and public is shown to be a blurry one. Although a picture of the Führer hangs in the Jordan house, for instance, when Nelly's father is drafted into the Second World War, her mother exclaims, "The hell with your Führer!" (*KM,* 157). Near the end of the war, furthering its termination, the Allied bombers traveling overhead on their way to Berlin are heard by the Jordan family as they were heard by many German families; similarly, the Jordan family helps with the refugees fleeing west and subsequently become refugees themselves, only to experience the occupation at the hands of the Americans, then the British, and finally the Russians, who were to become their ultimate guardians. The degree to which private and public are intermingled is well captured in the sentiment expressed by Nelly and two of her girl-friends that "Germany's defeat had taken away their ability to laugh" (*KM,* 359).

Hence we see that Wolf, although not born early enough to be a voting member of the National Socialist Party, is nonetheless interested in the formation and deformation of her generation by the Third Reich. In pursuing the question of how she, in the fictional persona of Nelly, was able to be inculcated with the ideology of national socialism, Wolf poses larger questions about how the horrors of the Third Reich were able to occur. The narrator offers a speculative answer: "We'd rather make our hearts into a murderer's den than make our four comfortable walls into a robbers' cave. It seems easier to transform a few hundred or thousand or million people into nonhumans or subhumans than to change our views on cleanliness and order and coziness" (*KM,* 186). Christa Wolf retrospectively attempts to accomplish what many Germans have failed ever to accomplish—a critical assessment of her participation in the darkest period of her nation's history. In doing so she avoids what she views as "the mortal sin of our time"—"the desire to not face up to one-self" (*KM,* 377).

Rousseau's *Confessions* (1782–1789) offers an illuminating contrast to *Kindheitsmuster.* In his autobiography Rousseau is at pains to paint the most favorable possible picture of himself, frequently distorting what are known to be the actual facts of his life in order to do so, yet insisting throughout that what he is writing is true. By contrast, Wolf uses her autobiographical novel as a means of facing up to and disclosing to the world the childhood self she had been ashamed of and had kept buried for some 25 years before beginning the book. In the words of her narrator, she "mediates between present and past through writing . . . makes possible the confrontation between today's person and yesterday's person by means of the written word" (*KM,* 153–54). By recalling and rethinking the life of the "she" designating "yesterday's person," the "you" denoting "today's person" comes to a fuller understanding of who and what she is, reflected in her ability at the end of the book to finally say "I." Thus the narrator's earlier vision, experienced while she is in the hospital and fearful of not finishing the novel, appears to be realized: "The final point would be reached when second and third person would meet again in the first, or even better, would coincide. When it would no longer be a matter of 'you' and 'she,' but rather 'I' could be said openly and freely" (*KM,* 322).

Not concealment, but disclosure; not embellishment, but candor; not denial and repression, but avowal—one can hope that the work of enlightenment Wolf has accomplished in her courageous autobiographical novel will help to prevent similar horrors from occurring again in the future. But the memories remain. To reiterate the novel's opening, "The past is not dead; it is not even past" (*KM,* 9).

Chapter Five
Confronting German Romanticism

The Rediscovery of Romanticism in the GDR

Although a good deal of fantastic literature was published in East Germany during the 1960s, notably by Anna Seghers and Johannes Bobrowski, it was in the first half of the 1970s that techniques and themes common to German romanticism experienced their most wideranging renaissance among GDR writers. In addition to Christa Wolf, authors such as Sarah Kirsch, Irmtraud Morgner, Günter de Bruyn, Stephan Hermlin, Alexander Abusch, Franz Fühmann, and Günter Kunert experimented with the fantastic, the grotesque, the absurd, and elements of dream and fairy tale. East German aesthetic and political doctrine had traditionally drawn a direct line from romanticism to fascism, and a disregard for or even antipathy to romantic thought lies at the foundation of East German ideology, indebted as it is to thinkers like Hegel, Marx, and Georg Lukács.[1] In the early 1970s, however, writers and critics in the GDR began exploring the revolutionary potential of romanticism. In the formulation of Sara Lennox, they understood this rethinking of romanticism as a "polemical opposition to an economistic and deterministic conception of Marxism which overemphasized technological progress and material well-being to the detriment of the human subject's self-realization and fulfillment."[2]

The affinity that GDR writers felt for the romantics was deepened by the fact that the writers of that earlier generation, like artists in the GDR, suffered under strict mechanisms of censorship. To symbolize the reigning cultural policies in the GDR that ordained oppressive measures such as censorship, writers often choose Goethe. Since the historical figure in his role as towering man of letters had in fact occasionally shown a lack of sympathy toward his younger, less successful contemporaries, it is not surprising that GDR writers, in their return to romantic settings and themes, frequently hold up Goethe as the embodiment of the status quo, the one who establishes and adheres to convention. All these features appear in the works by Wolf that are most heavily indebted to romanticism, *Unter den Linden: Drei unwahrscheinliche Geschichten* (1974; Unter den Linden: Three Improbable Stories) and the novella *Kein Ort. Nirgends* (1979; *No Place on Earth*), as well as essays related to it. Before turning to these works, however, we should take a look at another important influence on them.

Wolf and Ingeborg Bachmann

Along with Anna Seghers, the East German writer whose significance as a role model for Wolf was discussed in chapter 4, the Austrian poet and fiction writer Ingeborg Bachmann (1926–1973) may be regarded as one of the most formative influences on Wolf as a writer. Wolf's essay "Die zumutbare Wahrheit: Prosa der Ingeborg Bachmann" (1966; "The Truth You Can Expect: The Prose of Ingeborg Bachmann"), which she wrote as the afterword to Bachmann's collection of stories entitled *Undine geht* (Undine Goes), attempts to describe Bachmann's existential unhappiness as well as her efforts to alleviate it. In writing about Bachmann's feelings of powerlessness toward a world that appears increasingly alien to her, Wolf seems to crawl inside the poet's head to understand her predicament, characterizing her as "wounded, but not defeated; grieving, but free of self-pity; suffering, but not in love with suffering."[3] For Wolf, Bachmann's work manifests a weariness with civilization, a skepticism toward the value of progress in general, a sense of alienation not only from others but from herself. In the retrospective light of Bachmann's suicide some seven years after this essay was written, Wolf's portrayal of her as "desperate . . . menaced . . . disturbed . . . and [desirous of] being saved" ("ZW," 180) shows just how prescient was her recognition of Bachmann's anguish.

Yet Wolf does not stop at a diagnosis of Bachmann's suffering but goes on to describe the older writer's attempts to combat it through her work. Virtually all of what Wolf says is applicable to herself. Wolf finds in Bachmann, for example, the "greatest subjectivity, but no trace of caprice, neither the caprice of sympathy nor that of exuberance, but rather a tense authenticity" ("ZW," 176). Similarly, like Wolf herself, in Wolf's view Bachmann defends the human claim to self-realization, the right to individuality and personality development, and the longing for freedom. Wolf particularly admires in Bachmann something that she too possesses: the desire to effect change, and, in Bachmann's case, the search for a new language to help achieve this goal. Finally, just as Wolf's work endeavors to uphold humanistic values against a communist system that in many ways undermines them, Bachmann attempts to defend similar values against the "all-embracing destructive drive of late capitalist society" ("ZW," 185).

Although Wolf does not write in detail in this essay about individual techniques in Bachmann's stories, such as her use of the fantastic, which were to be influential on Wolf's own writing, in formulating what she regards as Bachmann's achievement Wolf offers an eloquent definition of the writer's task: "To acknowledge what is true—to make true what should be true"; "To become seeing, to make others see" ("ZW," 172, 174). Here Wolf indirectly gives voice to the objective of her own enterprise as a writer.

"Unter den Linden"

The mere existence of Wolf's story "Unter den Linden" demonstrates her toughness in the face of ideological adversity: as she notes in a diary entry of 26 June 1967 with reference to the difficulty that *Nachdenken über Christa T.* encounters with the censors, "One of the censors [who rejected the manuscript] assumes that I will now stop producing. I'm not going to do them that favor. Began 'Unter den Linden.' "[4] Given this background, it is not surprising that the story makes a critical comment on the repressive and restrictive measures adopted by the East German regime.

Possibly as a means of making this critique more palatable to the censors, Wolf cloaks it in a dream narrative. The title announces what is in effect the main character in this narrative, the former East Berlin's most famous boulevard. The story is framed by the first-person narrator's comment that she had avoided Unter den Linden for some time until it appeared to her in a dream, so that she is now able to talk about it, and the bulk of the story consists of her report of her dream to an intimate male friend who is frequently addressed in the second-person familiar form. The function of the dream as a key that unlocks the narrator's mental barrier to the boulevard is reminiscent of Freud's notion of the "return of the repressed," and as has been noted, the situation of a speaker telling her dream to another is analogous to one of the central practices of Freudian analysis.[5] The question thus arises: why had the narrator sought to avoid Unter den Linden, and how has her dream helped her overcome that block?

To answer this question it will be helpful to notice the ways in which the story weaves together elements of dream and reality. Details point to

a very specific geographic and temporal locale—contemporary down-
town East Berlin in June; although the narrator claims that the Unter
den Linden that is renowned as an east-west axis and the one that
appeared in her dream have "nothing to do with each other,"[6] in fact
many of the sites located on or near the famous boulevard are mentioned in her dream, such as the State Opera, the statues of Alexander
and Wilhelm von Humboldt, the guard station, the Academy of Sciences, the Friedrichstrasse, the Oranienburg Gate, the State Library, the
Alexanderplatz, the television tower, Marx-Engels Square, the Charlot-
tenstrasse, the Linden Hotel, the Dorotheenstädtische Cemetery, and
various well-known cafés and bars.

On the other hand, many other elements in the tale the narrator
recounts clearly mark it as a dream narrative, for example characters
who metamorphose into other characters, who disappear instantly, or
who look uncannily familiar; sudden panic attacks; wish-fulfillment
images; authority figures who turn out to be lacking in power; remnants
stemming from the day's activities and from earlier parts of the dream;
and details that are presented and then modified. The narrator repeatedly refers to the dream in a self-conscious fashion, observing that she
cannot explain it, that she knew in the dream that she was dreaming,
that she has a dream censor, and so forth. But because she often reports
the events of the dream almost as if they had actually occurred, the line
between fantasy and reality becomes fluid. As she paradoxically tells her
listener, "So that you'll believe me, I am now going to blur the boundaries between the credible and the incredible" (*GE,* 62). One of the most
striking examples of this technique is her description of her diving into
the fountain at the State Library and lying on the bottom of the pool.
While the reader knows that such an act is realistically impossible, the
technique used in narrating it inclines one to "believe" it.

This kind of hesitation between certainty and uncertainty about a
supernatural occurrence links "Unter den Linden," at least in tone, with
the fantastic mode as conceived by Todorov, which was discussed in
chapter 3. As mentioned earlier, the introduction of elements of dream
and the fantastic is part of the return to German romanticism that
occurs among many GDR writers in the 1960s and 1970s. But the cre-
ation of a dream narrative also places Wolf in a tradition stemming
above all from August Strindberg, the Swedish dramatist whose "dream
plays," externalizing unconscious thoughts and impulses as characters,
or unconscious wishes and fears as events, onstage alongside "realistic"
ones, revolutionized theater in the early twentieth century; the notion of

the dream play, with which playwrights like Maurice Maeterlinck in France at the turn of the century also experimented, was enormously influential for the writers, painters, and filmmakers of German expressionism and European surrealism.

It goes without saying that the fantastic techniques of "Unter den Linden," with their roots in romanticism and modernism, represent another marked departure on Wolf's part from the aesthetic doctrines of socialist realism. This break occurs on a thematic level as well. The story's critique of the GDR regime emerges despite the dream framework. East German society is depicted as pervaded by secrecy, deception, lies, and spying. This atmosphere is most evident in the dream subplot focusing on the narrator's friend Peter, a historian who was talked out of his original dissertation topic because it was politically unacceptable and who is now being observed and pursued, no doubt by the State Security Service (Stasi), or Secret Police. As we now know, by the time she wrote this story Wolf had had firsthand experience with the power of the Stasi, having provided information to the Secret Police as an informant between 1959 and 1962.

Moreover, in her dream the narrator herself is a defendant in a trial, and there is much talk of evidence, witnesses, testimony, and attorneys. It is possible that this sequence owes its existence to the guilt that Wolf may have felt because of her activity as a collaborator with the Stasi. In any case, the treatment of this element of the story, especially the narrator's feeling that her prosecutors intend to convict her, is reminiscent of Kafka's narratives, with which "Unter den Linden" has often been compared. As Hans-Georg Werner notes, however, Wolf's story differs from Kafka's prose works in that the law in "Unter den Linden" is not of metaphysical but of human origin and in that Wolf's tale ends not in self-alienation but in self-realization.[7] The latter observation refers primarily to the climax of the narrator's dream, in which she sees a woman who looks exactly the way she would like to look and who arouses piercing envy in her until she wakes up and recognizes the woman as herself, whereupon she realizes that she had been summoned by the court in order to find herself. The question posed earlier has now been answered: having learned through her dream that the intention of those pursuing her was benevolent, the narrator no longer needs to avoid Unter den Linden and is free to talk about the experience.

Yet much in the story undermines a one-sidedly optimistic interpretation. It is typically argued that the narrator's process of self-realization is achieved by her awareness of the importance of love. Other pieces of the dream concern the narrator's love for a surgeon whom she calls only "Mr. Unnamed" and the passionate relationship between Peter and an attractive blond, who blurs together with a girl who misses three months of lectures without an excuse because of her love for her instructor; near the end of the story the narrator claims that for people like her "the only connection with the world is, unfortunately, through love" and that she "cannot postpone love" (*GE,* 94). But the dishonesty that the story associates with the East German government is mirrored in these private relationships as well: we learn that Peter's affair with the girl began while he was married and that she secures a fraudulent excuse for her absences.

In light of the web of secrecy and lies that envelops both the private and public figures in the narrator's dream, her statement, made both at the beginning and at the end of the story—that "Above everything else we appreciate the pleasure of being known" (*GE,* 54, 96)—takes on an ironic cast. And yet, as we know from *Nachdenken über Christa T.* and other works, both love and the attempt to know and be known are endeavors to which the humanist Wolf ascribes paramount importance. "Unter den Linden" argues for the value of these endeavors at the same time as it demonstrates how difficult they are to achieve. From beneath the story's romantic, fantastic surface, an intensely realistic message emerges.

"Neue Lebensansichten eines Katers"

In the case of the second story in the collection *Unter den Linden,* "Neue Lebensansichten eines Katers" ("The New Life and Opinions of a Tomcat"), Wolf's debt to German romanticism is overt. The device of casting a clever cat as protagonist enjoyed great success in Ludwig Tieck's play *Der gestiefelte Kater* (1797; *Puss in Boots*), which presents the older fairy-tale material in a self-conscious manner typical of German romanticism. But as Wolf's title indicates, her explicit point of departure is the two-volume novel *Lebensansichten des Katers Murr nebst fragmentarischer Biographie des Kapellmeisters Johannes Kreisler in zufälligen Makulaturblättern* (1819/1821; Tomcat Murr's Views on Life, Together With a Fragmentary Biography of the Music Director Johannes Kreisler, Preserved on Random Sheets of Scratch Paper) by the romantic writer E.T.A. Hoffmann, in which Murr openly acknowledges his debt to Tieck. Considered by many to represent a high point of the romantic novel, Hoffmann's work is two-pronged, consisting of Murr's autobiography alter-nating with fragmentary pieces of Kreisler's biography, which were supposedly published inadvertently with Murr's narrative because the cat used pages from it as blotting paper and as a writing pad in composing his own story. The memoirs of the vain, hypocritical tomcat serve as a vehicle for parody of the bildungsroman, or novel of development or self-cultivation, a prominent form of the German novel in the eighteenth and nineteenth centuries; the parts of Hoffmann's novel focusing on Kreisler and his difficulties at a petty court explore the problem of the artist's alienation from society, which is one of the foremost themes in German literature.

Wolf's tale transplants these themes to contemporary East Germany and recasts them in a mode combining fairy tale and science fiction—a striking blend indeed. The lofty status that the arts possessed for romantic writers is occupied here by science; the Kreisler figure of Wolf's story, Rudolf Walter Barzel, is not an artist but rather a 45-year-old professor of applied psychology. The titular tomcat, here called Max, who belongs to the Barzels, is as narcissistic and spoiled as his predecessor Murr, boasting for example that he can experience "three complicated mental-psychic processes at the same time" and that "nothing human is foreign to me."[8] The human scribe in this instance is Barzel's teen-aged daughter Isa, into whose diary Max inserts his memoirs.

The story contains numerous other echoes of German romanticism and its context. In keeping with the self-conscious mode so prevalent in romantic literature, Max is aware of his "great ancestor" Tomcat Murr; the romantic era is further evoked by the name of a neighbor's female cat, Napoleon. These references are of course ironic, highlighting the disparity between the idealistic and heroic aspirations of the earlier era and the philistinism, in Wolf's view, of middle-class life in East Germany. Similarly, the book Max is planning to write, *A Guide for Adolescent Tomcats in Dealing with Humans,* suggests that the emphasis on transcendence and the power of the imagination so prevalent in romantic literature has been replaced in East German culture by a preoccupation with self-help.

Wolf's mockery of the self-help impulse is only one aspect of the story's satire, which, like Hoffmann's satirical attacks in his Murr/Kreisler novel, is multipronged. The critique of both private and public life in East Germany found in "Unter den Linden" is continued here, albeit in a lighter vein. A satirical attitude toward marriage is manifest in the portrayal of the Barzels; in the face of her husband's impotence Mrs. Barzel finds solace in crime novels, chocolates, and brandy, and eventually both partners begin spending nights away from home. The case of neighbors who continue living together after their divorce in an apartment where the former husband happily tolerates visits by his ex-wife's new boyfriend might be read as a latter-day realization of the doctrine of free love expounded by a number of German romantic thinkers; in any event it exemplifies the way in which the story's unhappy characters endeavor to live up to its epigraph, cited from Hoffmann's Murr/ Kreisler novel: "The more civilization, the less freedom, and that's the truth" (*GE*, 97).

And yet the main object of Wolf's satire appears to be the misguided nature of these characters' attempts to find happiness, above all in cybernetics. Barzel and his colleagues, the one a nutritionist and physiotherapist, the other a cybernetic sociologist, are working on a project designed to achieve Total Human Happiness, or the abolition of tragedy, which they refer to in top-secret fashion by its (German) anagram TOMEGEL; currently they are focusing on a crucial subdivision of TOMEGEL, SYMAGE, or System of Maximum Health of Body and Soul. Max feels privileged to live in the house of the system's inventor, where the cat can study the countless index cards on which the scientists have filed the categories that they believe constitute all factors beneficial for or detrimental to human health.

In this grotesque system Wolf mocks the notion that human life can be programmed and rationally controlled. Her satire finds a comic climax in Max's attempts to throw the SYMAGE into disarray; he inserts a card labeled "Parental Love" into the card case designated "Dangers Caused by Civilization" and files the card "Acquired Marital Impotence" under the category of "Stimulants." As in Hoffmann, the device of a self-possessed tomcat who prides himself on his education functions as a means of critiquing the reigning notion of *Bildung* or mental cultivation, in Wolf's case, the regimented, doctrinaire education received by children in the GDR. Wolf also takes a stab at East German aesthetic doctrines, specifically, at the socialist realist ideal of the positive hero, in Barzel's drunken promise at the close of the story that his computer Heinrich, which he uses to process the voluminous data for the SYMAGE project, will in the future be "positive."

In the end the story's Rousseauian epigraph, condemning civilization in favor of freedom, is successfully realized only in the life of its tomcat narrator, who eats and sleeps as much as he likes, defecates at will, and has sex whenever he wishes. Yet the story's suggestion that the utopian ideal of a free, uncivilized way of life is viable only for animals must be read in the context of Wolf's critique of the notion that human behavior can be rigidly categorized, normalized, and controlled. Somewhere, the reader infers, there must be a happy medium between these two extremes, and it is this middle ground that Wolf advocates.

Wolf and the Women Romantics

In the second half of the 1970s Wolf's return to German romanticism is significantly influenced by two developments: the so-called Biermann affair and her increasing interest in women romantic writers. The dissident poet and folksinger Wolf Biermann (b. 1936) possessed a deep-seated commitment to a better communism that manifested itself in his songs, which were often highly critical of the GDR regime. Expelled from the Socialist Unity Party in 1963, he was forbidden to perform in the GDR from 1965 on. Following a concert in Cologne in November 1976, he was expatriated. The following day a number of East German writers, including Sarah Kirsch, Stephan Hermlin, and Christa and Gerhard Wolf, horrified by this action on the part of the government, published an "Open Letter" in the party newspaper asking the government to rethink Biermann's expatriation. To Wolf's great disappointment, not only was Biermann not allowed back into the country, the government campaign against him and those who had signed the petition was accelerated, and Gerhard Wolf was expelled from the party. The shock was so great that Christa Wolf suffered a heart attack, and in December 1976 she, along with GDR writers Ulrich Plenzdorf, Jurek Becker, Sarah Kirsch, Günter de Bruyn, and Volker Braun, were expelled from the executive committee of the Berlin chapter of the Writers' Union of the GDR. Early in 1977 Christa Wolf herself received a sharp reprimand from the party.

It is not difficult to imagine the feelings of disillusionment and entrapment Wolf experienced at this time in her life. She had already encountered many references to early German romantic writers often considered marginal or "endangered"—Friedrich Hölderlin (1770–1843), Heinrich von Kleist (1777–1811), and the poet Karoline von Günderrode (1780–1806)—in the writings of her great model and mentor Anna Seghers, who defended these writers against the more strictly Marxist position of Georg Lukács. The more Wolf learned about the early nineteenth century in Germany, the more she recognized similarities between the oppressive political situation of that era and conditions reigning in the GDR. As subject matter for her writing, the romantic period seemed well-suited to her disillusioned frame of mind.

Wolf's feelings of affinity with Kleist and Günderrode, both of whom felt so alienated from society that their lives ended in suicide, eventually resulted in one of her most powerful narratives, *Kein Ort. Nirgends* (1979; *No Place on Earth*). The context of this novella may be illuminated by looking first at two major essays written prior to it, essays that familiarize us with the historical personages who appear in the novella: Wolf's preface to her 1979 collection of Günderrode's poems, prose, and letters, as well as documents by her contemporaries, and Wolf's afterword to her 1980 edition of Bettine von Arnim's *Die Günderode: Ein Briefwechsel* (1840; Günderrode: A Correspondence), Bettine's embellished edition of her correspondence with Günderrode.[9] I will discuss the Bettine essay first and then treat the Günderrode essay by way of introduction to *Kein Ort. Nirgends*.

Imitating the style so popular in the eighteenth and early nineteenth centuries, Wolf casts her essay on Bettine von Arnim (b. Brentano; 1785–1859) in the form of a letter, "Nun ja! Das nächste Leben geht aber heute an: Ein Brief über die Bettine" (1980; "Your Next Life Begins Today: A Letter about Bettine"). Bettine von Arnim, a prolific writer in her own right, is of special interest to Wolf because of her close association with Günderrode. As Wolf writes in the epistolary essay, Günderrode and Bettine met at the home of the well-known writer Sophie von La Roche, Bettine's grandmother. Bettine immediately attached herself to Günderrode, who was five years older and someone she looked up to. Conversely, Wolf's essay on Günderrode, "Der Schatten eines Traumes: Karoline von Gunderrode—ein Entwurf" (1979; "The Shadow of a Dream: A Sketch of Karoline von Günderrode") speculates about what Günderrode must have admired in Bettine: "The beautiful antitype to the well-trained, petty, pussyfooting social conformist, her pride, her love of freedom, the radicality of her thought and her hopes, her embodiment of utopia."[10]

This description captures Bettine in what Wolf marks off as the first phase of her life. She left this stage behind in 1811, when at the age of 26 she married the writer Achim von Arnim (1781–1831), a friend of her brother Clemens Brentano (1778–1842), likewise a writer. There followed 20 years of marriage, seven children, money problems, all manner of domestic annoyances, and, as Wolf observes, marital tensions as well. Yet Wolf appears even more impressed by the stage of Bettine's life that succeeded her period as a housewife and mother. Following

Arnim's death in 1831, when she was 46, Bettine von Arnim became a productive author. Her first book, *Goethes Briefwechsel mit einem Kinde* (1835; *Goethe's Correspondence with a Child*), the preface of which states that the book is "for good people, not for bad," exemplifies the preoccupation with Goethe, mentioned earlier, which virtually all nineteenth-century German authors, and many later ones, shared. Wolf cites Bettine's claim that during one encounter with Goethe she had lain down on the ground in front of him and insisted that he place his foot on her breast, so that she could feel his weight. Whatever the nature of her fascination with Goethe, this book made her famous overnight.

The tenor of Bettine von Arnim's work is well characterized by a statement of hers that Wolf uses as an epigraph to the afterword: "There is a lot of work to be done in the world; to me at least, nothing seems the way it ought to be."[11] The "world" in which she lived in the 1830s was, in Wolf's words, "the most petrified decade of the preceding century" ("BB," 291). And that is saying something, given the oppressive nature of the rest of the nineteenth century in Germany, or, many would say, of the history of German society and politics in general. In "Der Schatten eines Traumes" Wolf quotes Günderrode's description of the Germany of her day, the early nineteenth century: "Our cramped living conditions cut us off from nature, our narrow way of thinking prevents us from truly enjoying life, our forms of government preclude activity in the world outside. As tightly hemmed in as we are on all sides, our only choice is to turn our gaze heavenward or to turn it inward, brooding on ourselves" ("ST," 228).

Wolf also cites one of the more forceful and inspired commentators on German society, Karl Marx (1818–1883), noting that in his youth he considered social conditions in Germany to be "beneath the level of history" ("BB," 288) and mentioning his wry observation that the Germans had shared the restoration movements of modern nations without having shared their revolutions ("ST," 226). As the later phase of one of the restoration periods to which Marx refers, the 1830s, the "petrified" decade in which Bettine comes of age as a writer, is one of unusual political oppression. The Berlin journalist Adolf Glassbrenner, notes Wolf, claimed about those times that every Prussian seemed to have been born with an "inner gendarme" ("BB," 292). Police and censors were more active than ever.

This atmosphere of intimidation frightened even the socially committed Bettine von Arnim, who stopped writing her book about the lamentable conditions in which the poor lived and worked, in particular the textile weavers of Silesia (then part of northeastern Germany), because she was warned about possible recriminations. [The indigent and exploited conditions of the Silesian weavers in the 1840s were so notorious that they were later treated by such well-known writers as Heinrich Heine, who escaped the oppressive political climate in Germany by emigrating to France, in his poem "Die schlesischen Weber" (1847; "The Silesian Weavers") and Gerhart Hauptmann in his play *Die Weber* (1892; *The Weavers*).] Not to be silenced, however, Bettine continued working on a book in which she addressed herself directly to the authorities in depicting the shocking condition of the poor in Hamburg, *Dies Buch gehört dem König* (1843; This Book Belongs to the King), a book that at the time and even subsequently was regarded as irreligious and radical.

It is not difficult to understand why Wolf recognized similarities between the first half of the nineteenth century in Germany, especially the 1830s, and the postwar period in East Germany, and between the writers of that era and herself. These similarities are capsulized in the analogy between the case of the so-called Göttingen Seven and that of Wolf Biermann. The Göttingen Seven were seven university professors, among them the Brothers Grimm, who drew up and signed a petition of protest when in 1837 the local king revoked the constitution and released them from their oaths of allegiance to it. The seven professors were dismissed from their positions.

Always believing that the oppressed are in the right—in the opinion of her sister Gunda ("BB," 299)—Bettine fought vigorously on behalf of the Göttingen Seven. According to Wolf, however, Bettine experienced a moment of sudden insight into the "perverse separation between the morality of the state and the morality of everyday life" ("BB," 308)—a split that was painfully evident to Wolf in her own country during the 1970s as well, especially following the Biermann affair. Formulating matters even more starkly, Wolf writes with reference to Günderrode, "Unlike us she was not prepared by the history and literature of the next 170 years for those evil transformations that the reigning moral code effects in those who subordinate themselves to it" ("ST," 279–80).

Wolf's feelings of admiration and affinity for German writers from the first half of the last century are everywhere evident in the essays on Bettine and Günderrode. She has high regard for the passion with which Jakob Grimm composed the response to his dismissal from the University of Göttingen, she is enthusiastic about much of Bettine's prose, and her enthusiasm infuses an unprecedented color and vigor into her own style in recapturing these writers.

Wolf's strong engagement with romantic writers is perhaps most apparent in her descriptions of the close friendship between Bettine and Günderrode, which she almost seems to envy. Proceeding above all from Bettine's *Die Günderode: Ein Briefwechsel,* a free rendering that may best be called an epistolary novel, Wolf interprets the friendship as a love relationship. Yet it is an alliance between two significantly different temperaments. Attempting to put her finger on the differences, which resulted in the early demise of one woman and the tough survival of the other, Wolf observes that, whereas Bettine surrendered herself completely neither to love nor to art, Günderrode tried to do both—an endeavor that for a woman of her era (and of virtually all eras) was doomed to fail. As Wolf writes, "[Günderrode] was not only, as a woman, subject to the middle-class code of life; as a poet she subordinated herself to the middle-class code of art, so that she was under the double compulsion of sensitive moral feelings and of a sensitive artistic conscience. She was driven to the point where the preconditions for a life tolerable to her became incompatible" ("BB," 285).

Günderrode's vulnerability was exacerbated by the political atmosphere in which she lived as an adult, the first decade of the nineteenth century. Wolf eloquently summarizes the situation of Günderrode's generation—those coming of age in 1800—in the Günderrode essay:

> They, the sons and daughters of the first generation of educated, middle-class Germans and of impoverished noble families who had become middle-class, had a choice between the crippling, oppressive practices of German petty princes and being conquered by Napoleon; between the anachronistic feudalism of petty German states and the compulsory introduction of overdue administrative and economic reforms by the usurper, who naturally stringently suppressed the spirit of the Revolution. If this can be called a choice, then it was one that suffocated action at its root, when it had barely been conceived. This generation was the first to experience fundamentally the phenomenon of not being needed. ("ST," 230)

Kein Ort. Nirgends

The passage just quoted at length captures the political background of *Kein Ort. Nirgends,* and it is helpful in reading the novella to keep this description in mind. Many other elements and episodes of the novella also appear in Wolf's Günderrode essay: Günderrode's life at a convent for unmarried girls from impoverished noble families; the importance for her of her poetry-writing and of poetry in general; her publication of a volume of poetry under a pseudonym that is later unmasked, enraging her; her wish to be a man; her love for Friedrich Karl von Savigny, a law professor who marries Bettine's sister Gunda; the flirtation he carries on with Günderrode even after his marriage; her suicidal existence, which reaches its predictable end.

In contrast to the essay, however, the novella focuses on one moment in Günderrode's life, a fictive afternoon party at the house of Clemens and Sophie Brentano in the town of Winkel am Rhein in June of 1804. The novella, in other words, attempts to portray the perplexing figure of Günderrode by means of an intensive, telescopic approach rather than taking the more extensive, expansive approach employed in the essay. The narrative alternates between dialogue spoken by figures at the party, the internal point of view of Günderrode, the internal viewpoint of Kleist, and comments by the narrator, which are at times indistinguishable from the words or thoughts of the two main characters.

At this point in her life Günderrode is involved in a (spiritual) triangular relationship with Savigny and Gunda and has not yet met Friedrich Creuzer, the married professor of classical philology in Heidelberg with whom she had a relationship and whose eventual spurning of her would be the catalyst for her suicide, and Bettine has not yet married Achim von Arnim. But by far the most significant difference between the subject matter of the essay and that of the novella is the dominant role in the latter of Heinrich von Kleist, the brilliant Prussian writer who committed suicide at the age of 34 in 1811.

The fact that Wolf chooses to interweave her depiction of Günderrode with a fictionalized portrayal of a male writer suggests that the author wants to explore the gender ramifications of the artist's alienation. This assumption is supported by the gender-typed language used to introduce the reader to Kleist and Günderrode at the party at which the bulk of the novella is set: "A man, Kleist . . . The woman, Günderrode."[12] However, the fact that the female writer Bettine von Arnim, only five years Günderrode's junior, was productive and survived into old age and that the male writer Kleist was defeated by life like Günderrode invites us to look beyond gender for the key to their malaise.

Close analysis of the text reveals many similarities between the temperaments of Kleist and Günderrode as Wolf fictionally recreates them. Both are depicted as hypersensitive, Kleist as highly sensitive to all sensory stimuli, especially auditory ones, and Günderrode as hypersensitive to light. Kleist's recollection of a question he had once asked his physician, Dr. Wedekind, who had treated him during a recent breakdown and, within the fictional frame of the novella, has brought him to the gathering at the Brentanos, is particularly striking: "Can you imagine a person, Doctor, who has no skin but has to go out among people, who is tortured by every noise, blinded by every glimmer of light, pained by the softest touch of air? That's how it is with me, Doctor. I'm not exaggerating" (*KN,* 40). Both writers are plagued by physical ills, above all intense headaches.

A main source—or result—of the malaise of both unhappy young writers portrayed in *Kein Ort. Nirgends* is their feeling of being split or torn, as the novella's imagery starkly conveys. One of the two epigraphs to the text records Günderrode's arresting fantasy: "But this is why it seems to me that I see myself lying in my coffin, and my two selves are staring at each other in amazement" (*KN,* 5); later she is described as being "tensely poised between her soaring nature and her highly restrictive living conditions" (*KN,* 17). Similarly, Kleist tells Dr. Wedekind that he suffers from the misfortune of being dependent on ties that suffocate him if he puts up with them and that tear him apart if he frees himself from them. Going hand in hand with their split psychologies (again, the relationship between the factors in play is more likely one of mutual cause and effect) is the fact that both writers are unhappy in love. With feelings of guilt and disillusionment Kleist recalls his former fiancée Wilhelmine, with whom he had broken off some years before; remembering early in the novella the dream about Savigny she had had that morning, Günderrode realizes that she can have nothing of him but "the shadow of a dream" (*KN,* 9).

As an extreme result of their multifaceted malaise, both writers lead a suicidal existence, that is, a life that they imagine they can voluntarily end if it becomes intolerable. In a somewhat sensational scene in the novella, Günderrode accidentally drops from her handbag the small dagger she always carries with her, and the other guests at the party are shocked to discover its existence. Like so much else in this carefully researched work, this detail is based on historical fact; the historical Günderrode did in fact carry a small dagger with her, and in the end used it as the means of her suicide. In another incident based on fact we learn that Kleist, in despair, had recently gone so far as to join the army of the military leader he most detests, Napoleon, so that he (Kleist) would be likely to die at the hands of British soldiers, but that this plan was foiled by Napoleon's decision not to send his fleet to England. That

Kleist, descended from a rigidly Prussian military family, would even consider an action like this tells us much about his state of mind at the time, and the plan's failure considerably worsened his depression; it was on his return from France to Germany that he broke down and came under the care of Wedekind.

Not surprisingly, both Kleist and Günderrode feel alienated from others; their unsociable behavior at the party, where they talk mainly to each other, is typical. Reflecting the actual attitudes of many romantic writers, mentioned earlier, a major object of the alienation both feel is Goethe, although their attitude toward him could more accurately be characterized as ambivalent. While revering his work, they regard him as embodying a degree of balance, harmony, optimism, and felicity that can only be possessed by someone whose life has been as blessed as his. As a man in harmony with himself and the world, he represents a clear antitype to themselves.

On a larger scale, the negative attitudes of Kleist and Günderrode toward the other guests at the afternoon gathering seem to typify their sense of alienation from society. Both are critical of the falseness they perceive in society. Günderrode confides to Bettine that she intends to think some day about what it means that the most serious, most painful things are conveyed to people in the form of masquerade, and she wonders "whether so many smiling mouths conceal a grave illness on the part of society as a whole" (*KN*, 27). In Kleist's opinion the members of these social circles "come together only to confirm each other in their views" (*KN*, 74–75), and he mocks the manner in which people use social gatherings as an opportunity to display their knowledge. He longingly imagines that the day will come when "things will be as they should be and people will be judged according to their worth and dignity instead of according to good manners, name, and social position" (*KN*, 53–54). Stating his critique more baldly, Kleist later claims that no one, at least not in Prussia, asks what would be beneficial for the crowd, or people at large. Behind these criticisms of the falseness, secrecy, and hypocrisy of German society in the early 1800s, it is not difficult to perceive Wolf's dissatisfaction with similar ills in the GDR of her day and her sense of alienation in the face of the growing rigidity of the totalitarian regime under which she lived.

If Kleist and Günderrode are similar in their sensitivity and suffering, they are also linked by their primary means of combating it. Revealing Kleist's thoughts, the narrator tells us that he only feels true life by writing and that he could endure everything but never to write again.

Günderrode confesses to Clemens Brentano that she must write, that she longs to express her life in lasting form. And yet despite all the similarities Wolf's novella is at pains to point out between these two unhappy contemporaries, some striking differences are evident, differences that do suggest some generalizations about gender roles. Kleist and Günderrode, male and female writer, are similar and different, or, as the narrator formulates it from the perspective of both of them during a walk they take along the river following the party, "Different down to the ground, from the ground up similar to each other" (*KN,* 109). The novella ultimately depicts Kleist as being doomed by his nature. He thinks at one point, "Oh, this inborn bad habit of always being in places where I do not live, or in a time that is past or is yet to come" (*KN,* 29); he later tells Wedekind, "Nowhere have I found what I was seeking" (*KN,* 68). Nonspecific malaise, melancholy, ennui, mal du siècle—this syndrome was to become widespread in nineteenth-century literature and art, although not always with such fatal consequences as it had for the historical figure Heinrich von Kleist. With Günderrode, things are magnified: she suffered the double burden of possessing a hypersensitive, melancholic temperament and being a woman in an extremely repressive era. Günderrode's description of women's lot to Kleist is eye-opening: "People forbid us early on to be unhappy about our supposedly imaginary sufferings. By the age of seventeen we must have accepted our fate, which is a man, and must take our punishment in the unlikely case that we resist. How often have I wanted to be a man, and longed for the real wounds that you bring on yourselves!" (*KN,* 112–13). Whether either condition alone—being a woman or possessing her particular sensibility—would have led to the same outcome is impossible to say; Wolf's point seems to be that both together virtually doomed Günderrode to self-destruction. Again, her words to Kleist are telling: "Not only the circumstances of my life but also my nature have imposed tighter restrictions on my behavior than yours have done on you, Kleist" (*KN,* 104).

Yet the novella's implications about the female sex are not entirely negative. Although Günderrode tells Kleist that her wishes are "boundless" (*KN,* 87), in the way of many women at the time she has learned renunciation and self-denial. In contrast to Kleist, who often slips into the role of enfant terrible, she recognizes the power and necessity of convention and conformity, and her behavior is consistently mature, poised, and sensible. Similarly, her belief in free will stands in direct opposition to Kleist's theory that our lives are governed by blind chance. And the

heightened sensitivity that is associated here with femininity is appreci-
ated even by Kleist, whom Wolf depicts as nothing if not self-involved.
To Kleist Günderrode seems to be endowed with virtually extrasen-
sory powers of perception, "as if she had an intimation of the terrible
contradiction on which the ruination of human beings is based. And as if
she could summon up the strength not to deny this rift but to endure it"
(*KN*, 81); as the narrator further notes from Kleist's perspective, "the
unhealthy pleasure in pointing out the levers and rods behind the
scenes—Kleist had never encountered this in a woman" (*KN*, 97). The
affinity between his soul and hers is hence deep and powerful. He finds
that "even when this woman is speaking to others, she seems to be
addressing him, and that she strikes him as the only real person among a
crowd of masks" (*KN*, 65). Since "something in this woman magneti-
cally draws confessions from him that leave him highly vulnerable" (*KN*,
105) and encourages him to talk about his hidden secrets and deepest
doubts, he imagines that she might be the "one person on the earth to
whom he could confide his misery" (*KN*, 99).

Yet while Günderrode's heightened powers of perception distinguish
her in Kleist's mind from the female sex as he has known it up to now,
in the last analysis he can only view her as a woman, and he remains
trapped in his preconceptions about women's roles; she could, he muses,
still find a husband, have children, forget her youthful unhappiness:

> The woman is suffering, Kleist does not doubt that, but suffering is
> woman's lot. She will become reconciled to it, even if it is harder for her
> than for most, Kleist grants her that—in this she is similar to his sister.
> But he tells himself: she is taken care of, whatever that may mean; she
> does not have to turn her thoughts to the most trivial demands of every-
> day life. The fact that she has no choice strikes him as a blessing. As a
> woman, she is not subject to the law of having either to achieve every-
> thing or to regard everything as nothing. (*KN*, 107–8)

Nor is Günderrode free of gender-typed thinking. At the party she
and Sophie Brentano remark on how childish men are, Günderrode
points out to Savigny that men have a habit of always seeing only themselves, and she tells Kleist that according to her observations, women's
lives require more courage than men's. The difference between Kleist's
and Günderrode's conceptions of gender roles is that the characters in
the novella bear out the truth of her generalizations, whereas the reader
is clearly meant to have distance on his. Günderrode's assessment at the
end of the novella of Kleist's malaise, while not strictly a function of his

gender, was at the time certainly more characteristic of men than of women: whereas she allows love to play a key role in her life alongside her poetry, in her opinion the only absolute value in Kleist's life is his work; he would not, she thinks, give it up for the sake of another person, and hence is doomed to unhappiness. The irony of this observation is that it is precisely the split between her loyalty to art and her longing for love that destroys Günderrode in the end. The malaise of both Kleist and Günderrode, then, is primarily a function of their temperaments but is exacerbated, even in the case of Kleist, by their gender; in a double sense, there is no place on earth for either of them. *Kein Ort. Nirgends* thus points forward to Wolf's more explicit experiments with gender essentialism in the 1980s.

No discussion of *Kein Ort. Nirgends* would be complete without a closer look at its innovative style. To an even greater extent than in *Nachdenken über Christa T.* this novella represents a translation of the montage technique into literary form. Wolf interweaves actual literary, biographical, and historical material into her fictionalized portrayal in a way that often makes it difficult to determine which details are "authentic," hence underlining the subjective nature of our perceptions of others and the complex elusiveness of human identity. This notion of "subjective authenticity" will come increasingly to dominate Wolf's oeuvre.

If we think of the text of *Kein Ort. Nirgends* as a kind of jigsaw puzzle, which is an appropriate metaphor because of both the work's difficulty and its structure, it should be noted that many of the "pieces" of the puzzle are quotations. In her close study of the quotations in the novella, Ute Brandes has distinguished three main categories:

1.   General quotations that might have been recognized by Wolf's contemporary East German audience; these citations frequently contribute indirectly to the characterization of Kleist or Günderrode.
2.   Identified quotations, for example lines taken from the work of a writer whose name is provided by the main characters themselves, such as Goethe; according to Brandes, these quotations often spark a discussion that "gives a twist to the content of the social conversation."
3.   Unidentified quotations from the works and letters of Kleist, Günderrode, and other romantic writers. These pieces of the puzzle form the documentary framework of the novella and contribute more than any other element to its subjective authenticity.[13]

The subjectivity of the narrative is heightened by the fact that it consists for the most part of thoughts and words rather than actions; the fragmentary and nonlinear nature of these thoughts and words contribute to the difficulty of the text. The nondramatic quality of the text is also intensified by its lyricism. To cite only two examples, Günderrode remembers her room at the convent as "filled with green twilight" (*KN*, 8); Kleist's recollection of his experience as a young man in the Prussian king's army, stationed near the Rhine, is literally lyrical: "How he moved toward the evening breeze and toward the Rhine and the waves of the air and the water resounded around him simultaneously, so that he heard a melting adagio with all its melodic phrases and an entire harmonic accompaniment" (*KN*, 19). Virtually all Kleist's perceptions of the river are rendered in a similarly lyrical fashion.

But the most striking feature of the novella is its narrative technique, which more than any other element reflects Wolf's sense of the subjectivity of perception. When not reporting direct dialogue, the narrative voice moves freely from the third-person "omniscient" point of view to the technique of free indirect style or narrated monologue, which assumes the third-person, past-tense form but is restricted to the inside perspective of a single character, i.e., the narrator enters the mind of a character but renders his or her thoughts in the third person. The viewpoint conveyed by this technique is often ambiguous, since it is sometimes impossible to tell whether an observation is being made directly from the perspective of the narrator or from the point of view of a particular character as reported by the narrator. Hence we move around from the narrator's story to the thoughts of Kleist to the thoughts of Günderrode without always knowing to what extent these thoughts are being mediated by the narrator. This ambiguity is occasionally compounded by a further confusion as to whether a thought belongs to Kleist, Günderrode, the narrator, or all three; thoughts seem to float, suspended, in the air.

To make these general claims more concrete: one example occurs at the Brentano gathering as Günderrode is accused of arrogance by Clemens Brentano; following her response we read the isolated fragmentary statement, "That we cannot count on being known" (*KN*, 28). The next paragraph moves into Kleist's mind and registers one of his impressions of Günderrode. The statement about being known could hence be made from Günderrode's point of view, from Kleist's, or from the narrator's. The same is true of the statement appearing late in the novella, also in isolation, in the midst of a discussion between Kleist and Günderrode about his play *Robert Guiscard*, which he had burned: "I only write because I can't help it" (*KN*, 116). According to the logic of the conversation, this statement is made by Kleist, but there is no explicit indication of this, and certainly the admission could apply also to Günderrode and, for that matter, to the narrator, insofar as the narrator is autobiographical. This narrator even goes so far as to ask at several points, "Who is speaking?" as if to remind the reader how similar the views of Kleist and Günderrode—and herself—are.[14]

With this brilliantly economic technique of ambiguous perspective, Wolf blurs the identity, or underlines the similarity, of her two main writer-protagonists and of her sense of affinity with both of them and emphasizes the subjective nature of speaking, writing, and reading. Donna Reed sees this fluid narrative voice as representative of the boundlessness of much modern writing by women; in her view Wolf realizes through her narrative style "a utopian communion of the kind she has found among women."[15] In both the fluidity of its style and its intimation of the special power of female community, *Kein Ort. Nirgends* anticipates Wolf's next full-length narrative, *Kassandra* (1983).

Chapter Six
Feminism, Pacifism, Environmentalism

Christa Wolf's commitment to feminism, pacifism, and environmentalism, all of which are intertwined in her thinking, does not emerge overnight. Feminism receives its first extensive literary treatment in Wolf's oeuvre in "Selbstversuch: Traktat zu einem Protokoll" (1974; "Self-Experiment: Treatise on a Report"), the theme of pacifism lies at the heart of *Kassandra* (1983; *Cassandra*), and environmentalism is the point of departure for *Störfall: Nachrichten eines Tages* (1987; *Accident: A Day's News*)—the three works on which this chapter will focus. However, intimations of these directions are present elsewhere. For instance, in the episode in *Kindheitsmuster* (1976) in which Nelly is working as a clerk in the village occupied by the Russians and is helping out with women being examined for venereal disease, the narrator observes that, "It was a significant experience. For the first time Nelly saw how women had to pay for what men had done!" (*KM,* 338). Similarly, when the Russian doctor examining the women vehemently proclaims that unmarried women should be virgins, Nelly realizes that she does not agree. In many ways feminism represents the culmination of the humanistic rethinking of socialism that motivates Wolf's entire oeuvre.

Wolf's uneasiness over the escalating desire of world powers to rearm themselves, often with atomic weapons, following the Second World War appears at least as early as *Der geteilte Himmel* (1963), when Rita expresses her concern to Manfred that, "Already now there are more bombs in existence than would be necessary to blow up the earth" (*GH,* 177). Likewise, in one of her essays on Anna Seghers, "Glauben an Irdisches" (1968), Wolf writes, "Under the conditions of the atomic age the moral existence of the human race has become the precondition for its physical existence" (*GI,* 142). Subsequently Wolf has often expressed her fearful amazement at the fact that the existence of so many depends on the morality and good sense of so few, indeed, of a single individual with the power to press one fateful button.

Love and respect for the earth and a desire to see it protected rather than thoughtlessly squandered and ruined are also visible throughout Wolf's oeuvre, considerably before the so-called ecology movement arrived in Europe and the United States on a large scale. Even in early works like *Moskauer Novelle* (1961) and *Der geteilte Himmel,* critical note is made of the effects of industry on natural resources: the dirty, stinking water, white industrial foam, and poisoned fish in rivers into which waste products from chemical plants have been dumped; the air made filthy by the burning of brown coal. In *Kindheitsmuster* the narrator's daughter explains that the employees where she works receive milk for free because they have to handle a solution so unhealthy that it regularly gives her headaches. In the first of the *Voraussetzungen einer Erzählung: Kassandra. Frankfurter Poetik-Vorlesungen* (1983; Conditions of a Narrative: Cassandra. Frankfurt Lectures on Poetics), a series of lectures Wolf presented while holding a guest lectureship at the University in Frankfurt in 1982 about her travels to Greece two years earlier, the author makes reference with dismay to the acid rain and pollution that have poured over the faces of ancient statues in the Acropolis like tears, giving them in her view an air of mourning. Similarly, in the second Frankfurt lecture she notices with indignation that the city of Aulis is being destroyed by industrial installations and that Eleusis is being ruined by oil refineries. The environmental decay she witnesses in the cradle of Western civilization, whose artifacts had endured for thousands of years before they were exposed to industrial pollution, leads her to wonder whether human life will survive into the future.

The interrelation of pacifism and environmentalism is evident for example in the conclusion of Wolf's essay "Glauben an Irdisches": "The decision to produce [Seghers' oeuvre, with its commitment to pacifism] and the decision to fight for the improvement and continuation of the earth stem from the same roots" (*GI,* 143). And in her second Frankfurt lecture, Wolf links environmentalism and feminism by characterizing the domination of nature as masculine:

> "Learning through suffering": this appears to be the law of the new gods and also the way of masculine thought, which does not wish to love Mother Nature but to see through her in order to dominate her and to construct the astounding edifice of a world of the mind, far from nature and off-limits to women. Women are even to be feared, perhaps since— unbeknownst to the thinking, suffering, sleeping male—they *too* help arouse that guilty fear that pounds his heart awake. Wisdom against one's will. The gain of culture through the loss of nature. Progress

through suffering: the formulas, established 400 years before our era, that lie at the foundation of Western culture.[1]

As we will see, the concerns voiced in these passages are varied and expanded in "Selbstversuch," *Kassandra,* and *Störfall.*

"Selbstversuch"

As previewed in chapter 3, the story "Selbstversuch: Traktat zu einem Protokoll" ("Self-Experiment: Treatise on a Report"), was published in 1974, along with "Unter den Linden" and "Neue Lebensansichten eines Katers," in Wolf's collection *Unter den Linden: Drei unwahrscheinliche Geschichten.* It reappeared the following year as part of an anthology entitled *Blitz aus heiterm Himmel* (Bolt from the Blue), edited by the East Berlin-based author, translator, and editor Edith Anderson. The collection, which also contains stories by Günter de Bruyn, Sarah Kirsch, Karl-Heinz Jakobs, Rolf Schneider, Gotthold Gloger, and Anderson herself, as well as an essay by the literary critic Annemarie Auer, was the result of a call Anderson issued to GDR writers to create tales about sexual transformation. The mere premise of the anthology, in which every story depicts a man turning into a woman or a woman becoming a man or both, reflects the increasing interest in the fantastic among East German writers at the time, discussed in the previous chapter, and graphically testifies to the distance they have traveled since the days of strict adherence to socialist realism.

Although all the stories in *Blitz aus heiterm Himmel* criticize stereotypical gender differences that support male privilege, the authors employ a variety of narrative situations to convey this critique. On the most basic level, to depict convincingly the metamorphosis of a "she" into a "he" or of a male "I" into a female "I" poses particular technical challenges to the storyteller. Wolf in a sense avoids this problem by choosing to cast her narrative in the second person. In this "Treatise on a Report" a woman scientist adds to her official report about her sex-change experiment her candid explanation, addressed to the professor whom she secretly loves and who launched the experiment, of why she broke it off before her transformation to a man was complete. Although the drug she takes transforms her physically into a man overnight, the mental changes come only in stages, allowing her/him to be treated as a man and yet to perceive this experience as a woman. Written in the early 1970s but set in 1992, the story was cast as a futuristic or science-fiction tale. Subsequent developments in surgery have of course made the fantasy Wolf envisions a reality, demonstrating yet one more time the way in which life imitates art.

The narrative situation of Wolf's "treatise," in which a first-person female speaker addresses a man in the second person, functions as a textual model for the author's synthetic vision of the ideal relations between the sexes. But it also paradigmatically demonstrates her recognition of the power of gender roles. The fact that the first pronoun to appear in the text is "Sie"—the professorial "you" to whom the narrator is writing her appendix—announces her awareness of the need to engage the male Other in dialogue (albeit here one-sidedly, since the story does not contain his response).[2] Yet despite what some critics claim, this narrator is not unbrokenly feminine, but is rather the synthetic product of a dialectical process.[3] The story's tale of the blind Greek seer Tiresias is far from gratuitous. According to the version of the myth related by Wolf's narrator, Tiresias was changed into a woman for a time and then back into a man. Because of his unusual experience with both genders, Zeus and Hera, the king and queen of the gods, asked him which sex enjoys lovemaking more. When Tiresias responded that women experience far greater pleasure than men, Hera punished him for disclosing this well-kept secret by blinding him, but Zeus took pity on him and gave him the gift of prophecy. Like Tiresias, the narrator of "Selbstversuch" has been "on the other side," has experienced the opposite gender and left it behind.

In relating the genesis of the narrating subject "Selbstversuch," like so much of Wolf's other work, demonstrates "the process of becoming a subject," the process she believes prose fiction should nurture in the reader.[4] Concomitantly, the story of how the narrating "I" of "Selbstversuch" comes into being manifests the author's much-discussed notion of the "difficulty of saying 'I'," thematized in *Nachdenken über Christa T.* and at the heart of her subsequent work. In "Selbstversuch," the difficult story of how the female scientist attained narrative subjectivity is bound up with her sliding gender identity, best grasped through a close analysis of the relationship between herself and the professor, between the "I" and the "you" of the text.

Scrutiny of this relationship reveals that the narrator's sex-change experiment is merely the culmination of wishes and tendencies she has had for some time. We learn that she had already conceived the idea of becoming a man fourteen years before, when the professor had mentioned the possibility of such an experiment during a lecture she was attending, and that she has hoped for the chance ever since. Having subordinated her personal life to her career, she is still single and childless at the age of 33, unlike the "typical" woman. In her appendix she notes to the professor that she was at the outset of the experiment "capable of summoning up masculine courage and manly self-control, each of which would come to be necessary in its own time" and that "I am easily equal to any of your male scientists."[5] Hence we find that the narrator's gender identity was blurred even before she undertook the experiment.

As her teacher and the object of her love, the professor is also the narrator's model. She wants to become what he is: a male scientist. Thus his story is crucial to an understanding of her sliding gender identity. And close examination discloses that "Selbstversuch" is as much the story of the "you" addressed as of the narrating "I." This feature of the second-person technique has been discussed by Michel Butor, whose novel *La modification* (1957) is one of the most extensive and best-known examples of second-person narrative. Making typological distinctions with regard to person, he writes that "It is here that the use of the second person appears, which in the novel can be characterized as follows: the one to whom one tells one's own story." In telling the story of the "you," he explains, the second-person narrative reveals something the "you" is hiding, is unable to narrate for himself. In the process the "you" is taught, and even judged, since the implied first person serves as a kind of conscience for the second. In Butor's words, "It is because there is someone to whom one tells one's own story, something about oneself that is unknown, or that at least has never been verbalized, that there can be a second-person narrative, which will accordingly always be a didactic narrative."[6]

Much of what Butor says about the novel applies to short fiction as well, and even though the implied first-person presence of *La modification* is not embodied in any character and the text does not constitute an address, there are nevertheless similarities between his thoroughgoing use of the second person and the narrative situation of "Selbstversuch." For instance, Wolf's second-person forms recount "true narrative action" as defined by Bruce Morrissette: "a single, unique past or present action. (For example, 'You could look out of your window and see . . .' is not narrative 'you.' 'Attracted by a sudden noise outside, you went to the window and saw . . .' *is* narrative 'you'.)"[7] Correspondingly, the narrator's formulation of her real reason for undertaking the sex-change experiment, for wanting to become a man like the professor, recalls

Butor's generic description of the second person: "All my good and bad reasons no longer carried any weight compared to the one that was sufficient in and of itself: that I wanted to find out your secret" (*GE,* 163). Having discovered through her brief experience as the man Anders (meaning literally "different")—named, appropriately, by his model the professor—what makes the professor tick, she now teaches her former teacher (and the reader) what he is unable to admit consciously to himself, unable to bring up to the level of language.

In teaching the professor what she has learned about him, the narrator constantly judges him, recalling the judgmental quality of the implied first person in *La modification.* She reproaches him for his scientific rigidity, evident in his "superstitious worship of measurable results" and his "fanaticism for justice" (*GE,* 159); for his impersonal coldness and calculated invulnerability—"You make every effort never to get caught. . . . Either you know all the answers or you are too proud to reveal your ignorance by asking" (*GE,* 159); and for his machine-like, "always-prepared-for-everything-attitude" (*GE,* 175): "Since you would never permit the term 'crisis,' we silently agreed on 'turning point' " (*GE,* 178). As Anders, the narrator comes to believe that these qualities of the professor are typical of men in general: "The partial blindness contracted by nearly all men began to affect me as well, for these days the unlimited enjoyment of privileges is no longer possible otherwise" (*GE,* 181); in her post-experimental voice she speaks for women in general in writing to the professor, "Above all else we value the pleasure of being known. But to you our demand is nothing but an embarrassment, from which you entrench yourself, for all we know, behind your tests and questionnaires" (*GE,* 174). Hence the desire to be known, which we have seen explored in *Nachdenken über Christa T.* and other works by Wolf, is presented here as a predominantly feminine quality.

The sliding gender identity evident in the preceding two quotations, in which a masculine "me" alternates with a feminine "we," manifests itself at other points in the narrative as well. Again speaking on behalf of women in general and *about* men in general, the narrator formulates the "secret" of the professor as follows: "that the activities in which you lose yourselves will not make you happy, and that *we* have a right to resist if you try to drag us into them" (*GE,* 181; emphasis added), yet proceeds only a few lines later to write, "*We* men, on the other hand, take the weight of the world onto our shoulders, nearly collapsing under its weight" (*GE,* 182; emphasis added).

A similar pronoun confusion characterizes the process by which Anders learns to redefine words in keeping with his new gender, here, the word "city": "For him—that is, me, Anders—it was a mass of inexhaustible opportunities. He—that is, I—felt dazed by a city that wanted to teach me that it was my duty to make conquests, whereas the woman in me had not yet forgotten the technique of displaying oneself and, where necessary, of giving in" (*GE,* 172). Obviously the technical reason for these instances of pronoun confusion is that the narrator alternates between an "I" that refers to his period as Anders and a post-experimental "I." But as the last example in particular suggests, the effect of such gender blurring is to underline the narrator's decreasing ability, in the course of his weeks as Anders, to identify with the masculine in general and the professor specifically.

As the professor's value as a model for Anders declines, Anders's own sense of identity as a man is steadily eroded. The point at which Anders says that he feels "as if he were at the movies" and the professor unthinkingly responds, "You too?" (*GE,* 184) can be regarded as the climax of Anders's education about the professor, since this revelation unmasks the professor as one who perceives and lives life only superficially. This flash of insight moves Anders to break off the sex-change experiment. Ironically, the single moment of complete identity between the "I" and the "you" of the story represents "the confidential admission of a defect" (GE, 185), leads the "I" to realize about the professor "that you cannot love, and you know it" (GE, 184), and causes him to move away from the masculine "you" and return to womanhood.

Yet only now, through this dialectical progression from femininity to partial masculinity to a state informed by both, has the "I" achieved authentic subjectivity; in learning the truth about the beloved, emulated masculine Other, the narrating subject has come to genuinely know herself, to be able to say "I." Her second-person narrative is the result. Instead of wanting to *be* the "you" of this text, as Anders, her goal is now a dialogue with him. She has progressed from loving the professor to understanding him to judging him to wanting to attempt a realistic mutual love that joins judgment and affection, a goal evident in her observation that, "You'll be surprised to learn that language can help me, with its origin in that amazing spirit that could express 'to judge' and 'to love' in one single word: *meinen,* 'to mean or think' " (*GE,* 171).

This didactic treatise ends not with an emphasis on gender separation but with a call for a synthetic reconciliation between the sexes. The story's penultimate sentence sums up the narrator's dialogic program: "Now my experiment lies ahead of us: the attempt to love" (*GE*, 185). The first-person plural, blending the female "I" and the male "you" into an androgynous "we," implies that for the narrator sexual love necessitates the dissolution of rigid gender boundaries. With this experiment of love, clearly set up as an alternative to the scientific experiment she has just undergone, the narrator will continue her education of the professor, begun in the treatise she has addressed to him: just as she has ventured into the masculine realm of science and even into the male gender, so must the professor allow the "feminine" activity of loving to encroach upon his imperviously masculine world.

Hence the common designation of "Selbstversuch" as "utopian" cannot refer to the sex-change experiment, which is, more accurately, a "left-brain utopia," as Nancy Lukens calls it; such utopias, she writes, "represent Hybris . . . , since they disregard essential elements of the whole picture of human life. . . . They create the illusion of progress toward perfection and thereby kill the ongoing process of life."[8] It is rather the story's conclusion that is utopian, in its suggestion that the answer is not to privilege one sex (men), and then allow women to "become men," or acquire these privileges too, but instead to encourage both sexes to appropriate features of the other and thereby become more human. To borrow a distinction from Wolf's narrator, the author's goal is "human or humane" and not "male or masculine" (*menschlich* versus *männlich, GE,* 173). By the time Wolf published *Kassandra* nearly a decade later, however, the utopian vision of the relations between the sexes with which "Selbstversuch" closes had been brought firmly down to earth.

Voraussetzungen einer Erzählung: Kassandra

Because of her status as a successful and celebrated writer, Christa Wolf enjoyed many more privileges than the average citizen of the GDR, whose movements were highly restricted. Among the benefits accorded her were generous travel privileges. In 1980, for example, Wolf traveled to Greece with her husband Gerhard. When she was awarded a guest lectureship at the University of Frankfurt two years later, she presented a series of five lectures dealing with this trip. The fifth of these lectures became the narrative *Kassandra,* published in 1983. Before we turn to that work specifically, to provide a context it will be helpful to look at the first four lectures, published together in the same year under the title *Voraussetzungen einer Erzählung: Kassandra. Frankfurter Poetik-Vorlesungen.* One of Wolf's main reasons for going to Greece, as she tells the reader, is to do research on the Trojan War in connection with *Kassandra.* But as a German writer traveling to Greece, she is also participating in a long and venerable tradition. German Grecophilia, or love of Greece, found one of its earliest and most enthusiastic exponents in the Greek scholar and archaeologist Johann J. Winckelmann (1717–1768), who in a history of classical art coined the phrase "noble simplicity and quiet grandeur" to characterize Greek art. Not surprisingly, in addition to the aesthetic qualities celebrated by Winckelmann, in their idealization of Greece German artists discerned and emphasized features of Greek culture that were not widespread in Germany or were missing there altogether—a lack of social inhibitions, emotional and sexual expressiveness, lightness of heart, Mediterranean beauty and climate, and so forth.

Grecophilia survives through generations of German writers who, failing ever to reach Greece itself, continued to "search with their souls for the land of the Greeks," as the phenomenon is described by one of its most avid and best-known representatives, Johann Wolfgang von Goethe (1749–1832), in his play *Iphigenia in Tauris.* Other German writers whose works reflect a strong interest in Greek culture are Gotthold Lessing, Johann Herder, Friedrich Hölderlin, Friedrich Schiller, Heinrich Heine, Franz Grillparzer, Friedrich Nietzsche, Stefan George, and Thomas Mann. As we will see, however, especially in *Kassandra,* Wolf stands this tradition on its head.

Participating in another tried-and-true tradition in German literature, Wolf casts her first two lectures in the form of a travel report. Like many writers of such reports before her, she details her impressions of sites visited during the trip, kinds of food and drink consumed, other tourists, and the friends with whom she and "G.," as she refers to her husband, are staying. But Wolf's impressions bear the stamp of the unusually high level of sensitivity to which the reader of her works has become accustomed. She constantly makes comparisons, for example, between ancient Greece and the present, a process that leads her to conclude that some things never change and that when things do, they usually change for the worse. In a gesture that can now, in the wake of German unification and the absorption of East Germany into the West, be seen as prophetic, she criticizes the Western drive for prosperity that eradicates individualism.

Anticipating the narrative in which the Frankfurt lectures culminate, Wolf sounds the note of war and peace in a distinctly minor key. It is important to keep in mind that she is writing in 1980, when the danger of atomic war in Europe was at its height. Wolf's fears for Europe (and, one can infer, for Germany in particular), situated in the line of fire between the superpower rivals of the United States and the (then) Soviet Union, are typical of Germans' feelings of helplessness and vulnerability at the time. She begins the third lecture by quoting Sarah Kirsch's poem "Ende des Jahres" (Year's End), replete with images of atomic mushrooms, neutron weapons, speeches by the military of all countries. Wolf repeatedly opposes the good sense of the many to the folly of the few who control the means of annihilating them in a matter of seconds. As she points out, "The realization that the physical existence of all of us depends on the shifts in delusional thinking of a very small group of people, in other words, on chance, of course completely unhinges the classical aesthetic, knocks it out of its moorings, which in the last analysis are fastened to the laws of reason" (*VE*, 84).

For Wolf, an example of such "delusional thinking" is the American president's decision, on the anniversary of the dropping of the bomb on Hiroshima, to build the neutron bomb. This detail demonstrates the way in which she interweaves entries about her readings on Troy in her third lecture, a "work diary" (on *Kassandra*), with references to the liberation of the concentration camp at Dachau, the effects of the bomb dropped on Hiroshima, and the contemporary arms race. All of these events are linked, as products of delusional thinking, and for Wolf there is only one answer: disarmament.

As an interim solution, however, Wolf has another answer, a "valiant, if groundless, effort to create a shelter for free-floating reason and for oneself: literature" (*VE*, 84–85). Even in the face of such powerful forces of darkness as war, the Holocaust, and atomic power, Wolf maintains her humanistic faith in the ability of literature to elevate and bestow dignity. Specifically, Wolf is concerned in the third and fourth Frankfurt lectures with writing by women, which she views as a medium that "they place between themselves and the world of men" (*VE*, 90). In these lectures, which constitute Wolf's most important statements on the subject of women's literature, she defends the existence of a body of writing that is different because it is by women: "To what extent does 'feminine' writing really exist? To the extent that women, for historical and biological reasons, experience another reality than men do" (*VE*, 114).

Because the previous existence of women was, in Wolf's formulation, "unrealistic" (*VE*, 115)—because, prior to the twentieth century, women did not have access to higher education and the professions and were active not in society but rather in the domestic sphere—their writing is often confined to the small details of home and family. As if to illustrate this postulate, Wolf includes numerous such details of daily life in the Frankfurt lectures, as elsewhere in her oeuvre. We read about what she eats, about the cherry tree she sees from the window of her study in her house in Mecklenburg, and about the simple activities she enjoys there, such as carrying in wood, hanging up laundry, and frying fish. While precisely such attention to the banal details of everyday life has gotten on the nerves of many of Wolf's readers, it may also be attributable to a general fact about women's writing to which Wolf calls attention in the fourth lecture, which is cast in the form of a letter to a fellow female writer: "We have no authentic models. This costs us time, detours, mistakes; but it does not have to be a pure disadvantage" (*VE*, 146).

Through her own writing, which will serve as a model for subsequent women writers, Wolf is helping to remedy this situation. In *Kassandra*, she specifically offers a model for the rewriting of patriarchal myths and legends that have survived for thousands of years—in this case, the story of the Trojan War—from a feminist perspective. In Wolf's reinterpretation of Cassandra, the themes of pacifism and feminism come together. For Wolf not only views Cassandra as one of the first female figures whose fate prefigures what would happen to women for the next 3,000 years: "that they would be made into objects" (*VE*, 86); she also recognizes the bloody consequences of this process: "Turning a person into an object: is this not the principal source of violence?" (*VE*, 114).

Kassandra

Neither of the two classical treatments of the Cassandra legend to which Wolf refers—Homer's *Iliad* and Aeschylus's *Oresteia*—pays much attention to the figure of Cassandra. In Wolf's opinion Cassandra did not interest Aeschylus "the way the murderers interested him" (VE, 42), and her view of *The Iliad* is that "Everyday life, the world of women, only shimmers through in the gaps between the descriptions of battle" (*VE*, 91–92). By contrast, Wolf makes Cassandra the literal and figurative focus by writing the tale as a first-person narrative, or monologue, spoken by the title figure herself. In the course of her narrative, the reader learns, or is reminded of, the bare facts of her life: she is the favorite daughter among the numerous children of Priam and Hecuba, king and queen of Troy (in the late twelfth century B.C., the period in which the Trojan War is now presumed to have occurred); loved by Apollo, she was endowed with the gift of prophecy, but when she refused the god's advances, he decreed that no one would believe her predictions. She functions as a priestess who is especially valued for her ability to interpret dreams.

Wolf's narrative begins after the Trojans have lost the war and Cassandra has been given as a slave to Agamemnon, the commander of the Greek fleet. Returning with him to his palace in Mycenae, she foresees that she will be killed in a few hours, as will he, by his wife Clytemnestra. Hence this narrative constitutes her (extended) last words. Rather than predicting the fall of Troy, she tells the tale with the benefit of hindsight. Cassandra's monologue moves freely among thoughts and words, spoken and unspoken, of herself and others from before, during, and after the war. Yet despite the collage-like structure and nonlinear chronology, which we have seen Wolf use in several of her earlier works, certain dominant themes emerge. As we have also encountered in Wolf before, although never to such a graphic degree, these themes can be seen to exist in a dialectical relationship to each other: on the one hand, the mechanisms of patriarchy, above all the exploitation of women, the view that war and aggression are necessary, and the cult of the hero, and on the other hand a belief system that values sexual equality, feelings of community, caring, and love. As we will see, the narrative can be read on two levels: although the events it relates occurred more than 3,000 years ago, through her critical portrayal of patriarchy in the ancient world, she critiques its remnants in her own society.

The exploitation of women that Wolf regards as intrinsic to patriarchy is extensively illustrated in Cassandra, whose humiliations at the hands of men are multiple: she is forced to tolerate the Greek Panthous in bed, although he disgusts her; near the end of the war her own father gives her to Eurypylos as wife in return for his agreeing to fight on the side of the Trojans; and at the end of the war she is raped by Ajax the Lesser in the grave of the heroes, only to then be made a booty slave by Agamemnon, as mentioned earlier. And yet, as it is important to keep in mind, she has survived (thus far) to tell the tale, and to tell it the way she wants to, regardless of whether she will be "believed" or not. In this connection it is illuminating to view *Kassandra* in the context of a typology of women's writing about the female body conceived by Sabine

Wilke. Wilke claims that Wolf's works, above all *Kassandra*, span a spectrum that is occupied at one end by texts where the female body functions as the stage on which social structures are played out, often in the form of rape, and at the other end by texts in which the female body finds a voice and asserts itself, often in an act of liberation.[9] The presence of both poles of this spectrum in *Kassandra* reflects Wolf's awareness that the status of women, while clearly improved since Cassandra's day, remains ambiguous.

But the narrative's depiction of the exploitation of women does not stop with its title figure. Her beautiful sister Polyxena, who according to Cassandra is desired by all men, acts as a slave to her lover Andron and, after the lust of the Greek warrior Achilles has been inflamed by the sight of her, is used as a pawn and a decoy for the cause of the Trojans. And, in one of Wolf's many reinterpretations or even reversals of the conventional legend, Helen of Troy herself is portrayed as an object fought over by a series of men, a "ball tossed back and forth," as Wolf puts it in her fourth Frankfurt lecture (*VE,* 147). Wolf's Helen, rather than being the beautiful seductress who started the Trojan War, is stolen again by the King of Egypt after she is abducted by Paris, so that the Trojans no longer even have her. Yet they attempt to hide this fact in order to maintain her as a pretext in place of the actual reasons for the war, which are economic. The situations of Cassandra, Polyxena, and Helen are extreme illustrations of the fates of many other female figures in the narrative, which in many ways can be read as one long wail over the lot of women in an intensely patriarchal society.

From the perspective of Cassandra, a comparably lamentable feature of this society is the value it places on war. The narrative's relentless depiction of aggression, cruelty, and bloodshed has no parallel elsewhere in Wolf's work. In a gesture that places her squarely at odds with the long tradition of German Grecophilia discussed earlier, these features are associated above all with the Greeks. And in yet another reversal, the figure who had been for Homer the greatest of the Greek heroes becomes for Wolf "Achilles the Brute" ("Achill das Vieh"). The savage behavior of Wolf's Achilles includes strangling Cassandra's brother Troilus and then cutting off his head in the temple of Apollo; plundering villages, killing the male inhabitants and raping the women, and wantonly cutting the throats of the sheep and goats; tying the body of the Trojan warrior Hector, another of Cassandra's brothers, to his chariot and dragging it around the citadel until it is a "lump of raw meat" in revenge for the killing of his beloved friend Patroclus by the Trojans[10];

and butchering twelve prisoners, including two brothers of Cassandra, to sacrifice on the funeral pyre of Patroclus. Achilles' bestiality manifests itself not only in bloodthirstiness but also in insatiable sexuality; he is depicted as lusting after everyone and everything, male as well as female. Achilles' aggressive character and behavior, which are so extreme as to be grotesque, can be read as Wolf's nightmare vision of the destructive power of war. Yet she is interested in war and cruelty not for their own sake but in their psychological and physical effects, which she finds devastating. Achilles arouses passionate hatred in the priestess Cassandra; elsewhere in the text the embodiment of benevolence, she longs for "an abyss of contempt or oblivion" between Achilles and posterity (*K,* 93). As Cassandra acknowledges in a particularly gripping passage, war both promotes and reveals human cruelty: "We had to recognize that there are no limits to the atrocities that human beings can inflict on each other, that we are capable of ransacking someone's intestines and cracking his skull in our attempt to cause the greatest pain" (*K,* 139). War is also undermined in *Kassandra,* although not as graphically, by being linked with dishonesty: the Trojan War not only begins because of a "phantom" (*K,* 82)—Helen—but is finally ended by means of a ruse—the wooden horse filled with Greek soldiers that is brought into Troy through treachery.

An additional patriarchal institution that is laid bare in Wolf's narrative is that of heroism. The dismantling of Achilles as Homeric hero is the most extreme example of this process, but there are many others. When we first encounter Agamemnon, who had possessed a reputation as the great commander-in-chief of the Greek fleet, he is described as "whimpering" and "spewing" (*K,* 6). The myth of Agamemnon as manly hero is further deflated through the revelation that he has long been impotent, a detail that explains to Cassandra his "exceptional cruelty in battle" (*K,* 13). Similarly, in response to Cassandra's question about Iphigenia, the daughter Agamemnon sacrificed so that the winds would gain enough strength to send his ships to Troy to begin the war, he weeps "from fear and weakness" (*K,* 63) and insists that he had no choice. Cassandra's view of Agamemnon as a "weakling who lacked self-confidence" (*K,* 63) is paralleled by her opinion of her brother Paris, whom she repeatedly lambastes as weak, conformist, and hypocritical because of his refusal to admit, after bragging in public about how he would steal Helen away from her husband, that he has lost her to the Egyptian king. Again and again "heroism" is unmasked as a desperate effort to compensate for weakness, impotence, unmanliness.

After reading Wolf's *Kassandra,* one can never again read Homer's tales of the heroes of Greece and Troy in the same way as before. However, the most powerful critique of heroism is made not through negative characters but through a highly sympathetic one. Cassandra begins to have ambivalent feelings toward her lover Aeneas, whom she has adored, only when he begins acting in the interest of the royal family and subordinating his own personal desires to the greater good—in other words, when he begins acting like a hero in the classical sense. At the end of the narrative we learn that she has refused to accompany Aeneas on his journey to found "a new Troy" because she foresees that he is about to become a hero, and she cannot love a hero. She does not want to experience his "transformation into a statue." As she tells him, "We have no chance in an age that needs heroes; you knew that as well as I" (*K,* 160). Once again Wolf inverts our conventional way of seeing to make us see more clearly.

Cassandra's subordination of public values to private desires intimates the ethic that she counterposes to the patriarchal glorification of war and heroism. She laments the fact that the tablets of the Trojan scribes record the palace accounts, the grain, urns, weapons, and prisoners won and lost but omit any reference to the pain, happiness, and love experienced by the city's inhabitants. One of the maxims by which she lives is that "the failure to feel never represents progress and is hardly a relief" (*K,* 61); at the low point in the war she observes, "No, I was not insane; what I needed was calming down. Peace that was not the peace of the grave. Living peace. The peace of love" (*K,* 143). Her belief in the power of love is accompanied by compassion; after Achilles murders the Trojan prisoners, it is she who prevents Paris from having a band of Greek captives killed in return.

The ethic of love and benevolence in *Kassandra* is associated for the most part with women characters. The narrative even creates a geographical space in which this feminine ethic can be sheltered and nurtured, the caves at Mount Ida, where female slaves, women from outside the citadel, and other women gather to dance and commune. On occasion the gender differential that assigns a positive value to the feminine and a negative value to the masculine is made explicit. With reference to her father Priam, Cassandra remarks, "For the first time it dawned on me that the intimacy between us was based, as so often between men and women, on the fact that I knew him and he did not know me" (*K,* 60). Most acts of violence in the narrative are committed by male characters. In describing the scene in which Achilles strangles Troilus, Cassandra speaks of the "naked hideous male pleasure" (*K,* 88) visible in Achilles' face.

Not surprisingly, after witnessing this horror and many others, Cassandra avows that she will never again want to be a man and is thankful that she is allowed to be a woman. This claim, we will recall, stands in stark contrast to the fervent wish Günderrode expresses in *Kein Ort. Nirgends* that she were a man. Like her belief in the existence of "feminine writing," Wolf's increasing conviction that for biological and social reasons women are in general more benevolent and more emotionally expressive than men is significantly influenced by her readings in contemporary feminist theory, especially that written in France. In historical terms, it is worth noting that this emphasis on gender difference rather than on equality between the sexes marks a significant distinction between the nineteenth-century women's movement and current trends in feminist thought.

There are, however, notable exceptions to the dichotomy in *Kassandra* that values the feminine as positive and the masculine as negative. As one might expect, Cassandra's lover Aeneas is quite unlike the other male characters in the narrative, as is his father Anchises. Both exhibit a caring nature and are a source of comfort to Cassandra. Anchises, who carves figures that are believed to possess special protective significance, is adept at typically feminine activities such as weaving baskets and baking cakes.

Similarly, as soon as Cassandra makes the generalization that "all men are self-centered children," she corrects herself: "(And Aeneas? Nonsense. Aeneas is an adult)" (*K,* 12). Cassandra's passionate descriptions of the love between herself and Aeneas place their relationship alongside great literary loves such as that between Tristan and Isolde: Cassandra declares that she feels at one with Aeneas, that when she breathes the same air he does, life flows back into her body. Most significantly, as she recalls at the end of the narrative, throughout their relationship he has never pressured her, has always let her be her own person, never wanted to twist or change anything about her—until now, when the hero begins taking precedence over the sensitive man and he tries to order her to accompany him out of Troy. As has been observed, the female characters in *Kassandra* are more convincing than the male figures, who are portrayed as one-sidedly good or evil. In the world of aggression, cruelty, and bloodshed depicted by this narrative, Anchises and Aeneas, in whom the "feminine" attributes of benevolence, imagination, tenderness, and sensitivity are as evident as in any of the women characters, take on a decidedly utopian aura.[11]

Wolf's revelation in the third Frankfurt lecture that she is increasingly coming to view her *Kassandra* narrative as a roman à clef (*VE,* 119) is provocative and invites the reader to search for similarities. One of the most obvious might seem to be the ever-vigilant palace guard Eumelos: in his position as chief of security who has cast a net of surveillance over the entire city of Troy, he evokes associations with the head of the East German State Security Service or Secret Police (Stasi), which Wolf had ample reason to critique. Priam, the father who loves his daughter but mistreats and disappoints her, has been read as a veiled personification of the East German government.[12] In larger terms, the opposition between Troy and Greece has been seen as similar to the differences between the GDR and the Federal Republic of Germany.

Within this context, compelling parallels exist between the title figure of the narrative and the author herself. For example, like Wolf, Cassandra is exceptional, both in her own eyes and in the eyes of others. Similarly, we learn that Cassandra wants to exercise influence over people, a desire that is inherent in the enterprise of being a published writer like Wolf. And, just as we have seen Wolf again and again call attention to the subjective, multilayered nature of reality and to the importance of individual perception in interpreting it, Cassandra becomes aware that there are multiple realities. In this respect, as in so many others, her thinking differs from that of the Greeks, for whom there exist only "either truth or lies, right or wrong, victory or defeat, friend or foe, life or death" (*K,* 124). It seems less important to decode possible hidden allusions to particular individuals whom Wolf may have been targeting or to simply equate Greece with West Germany and Troy with the GDR than to recognize "the Greeks" in general as a powerful symbol of a black-white mentality that prizes exploitation, aggression, materialism, and violence—all things that Wolf deplores.

A further similarity between Cassandra and her creator lies in the fact that Cassandra often brings isolation or ill treatment on herself because of her pursuit of honesty, justice, or fair treatment of others, such as when she wants the truth about Helen revealed or when she tries to prevent the Trojans from using her sister Polyxena as sexual bait to trap Achilles. We are reminded of the East German government's punitive treatment of Wolf and her husband after she signed the petition protesting the expatriation of Wolf Biermann. Wolf's critical vision, constantly sensitive to the ways in which her society could be improved, is reflected in Cassandra's rhetorical question, "But what kind of world were we living in then?" repeated throughout the narrative like a refrain. Especially striking in connection with Wolf's critical vision is Cassandra's assertion that, "I did not want the world the way it was, but I wanted to serve devotedly the gods that ruled it" (*K,* 48)—which can be read as an indirect formulation of Wolf's project as a thinker and author as we have encountered it throughout her work: while she found much that was wrong with the East German state, she remained committed to the idea of socialism until its dying breath.

Störfall: Nachrichten eines Tages

Just as Wolf's commitment to feminism and pacifism come together in *Kassandra, Störfall: Nachrichten eines Tages* (1987; *Accident: A Day's News*), interweaves the themes of pacifism and environmentalism. Like *Kassandra,* this narrative is a monologic collage of thoughts and memories of a first-person narrator with autobiographical underpinnings. Here, however, the "news" announced in the title is quite contemporary and refers to two major events in the narrator's life that converge on a day in late April 1986: the far-reaching repercussions of a fire in a nuclear reactor block in a place identified only as being 2,000 kilometers away (but which is clearly Chernobyl) and an operation in which a tumor is removed from her younger brother's brain. Written between June and September 1986, as the text explicitly indicates, the narrative recalls the day of the surgery by recording the narrator's fears, fantasies, recollections, and activities; these are intermingled with pieces of information she gathers about the repercussions of the nuclear meltdown, the location of which is not so far away as to leave her village unaffected. Moving freely back and forth between past, present, and projected future, the text includes imaginary conversations the narrator carries on with her brother, the words of conversations she has on the telephone and with neighbors in the village whom she meets while running errands, her encounter with a family looking for their residence during the war years, quotations from literary works and folk songs, and descriptions of her work in the garden and of other daily tasks. Because, as we learn, the narrator has been alone—without a "certain someone"[13]—for several days, she has begun, quite literally, to talk to herself, and much of the narrative does possess the personal, open quality of a conversation with oneself. In this quality, the book reflects the direction she sees writing to be increasingly taking, as she imagines telling her brother, "In writing, brother—since you asked—we have to play the role of the writer more and more and at the same time to shed our mask, to let our authentic self shimmer through. . . . A day like this, paradoxical in its repercussions, forces us, forces me to make personal things public" (*S,* 92). In *Störfall* the narrator "makes the personal public" to a greater degree than ever before in her work; although we have seen Wolf attending to the small details of daily life from her early stories onward, in this text such details occupy a narrative weight comparable to that of the "news" the narrator receives. We read of her singing in the shower, measuring out the coffee, slicing bread, chopping herbs, peeling potatoes, pulling out nettles by the roots, anticipating fried zucchini with garlic sauce in the summertime, reading her mail, taking a nap, crying because of nerves, doing exercises, confronting ants in the kitchen, drinking wine, watching television, and so on.

Although these kinds of details have been criticized as trivial and superfluous to the central action of the narrative, they make more sense when one considers the narrator's thought about "Life as a series of days. . . . The lasting pleasures. The framework that carries life even through dead times" (S, 13–14). Just as the steady progression of her daily routine, piece by piece, helps the narrator through a double crisis that she must bear alone, reading about this process can, ideally speaking, bring similar comfort to Wolf's reading public.

For the reader familiar with Wolf's life, the inclusion of such private details enhances the autobiographical character of *Störfall,* as do many other elements of the narrative. Wolf herself does of course have a younger brother, and numerous details the narrator recalls from her childhood and youth correspond to similar ones that appear in the autobiographical novel *Kindheitsmuster,* such as the Mecklenburg town where she and her brother both had typhoid fever as children, the incident in which she dislocated his shoulder, or the machine-gun fire from low-flying planes that she often had to dodge at the end of the war. The cherry tree that the writer of the Frankfurt lectures can see from the window of her study makes an appearance here too, thereby identifying the narrative voice of *Störfall* fairly definitively.

But what lifts this narrative out of the realm of a personal, diary-like account of "a day in the life" and indeed gives it universal significance is its exploration of the Janus-faced nature of science: the two pieces of news dominating this day graphically illustrate the destructive and constructive potential of science. In the course of the narrative the narrator learns various pieces of "news" about the devastating effects of the nuclear meltdown: the inhabitants of Kiev are being evacuated, in Sweden the radioactive contamination of the ground is rising, and even in her area, although 2,000 kilometers from the accident, people are being advised not to buy fresh milk or green vegetables, and the water and fish are suspect as well.

Wolf's narrator emerges as a spokesperson for the powerless population in the face of this disastrous, impersonal accident. Rendered a victim like her neighbors, her countrymen, and everyone else in the vast contaminated space surrounding the site of the meltdown, she advocates renouncing nuclear technology if its effects cannot be controlled with certainty. In lamenting this state of affairs the narrator is sensitive to the "connection between killing and inventing" (*S,* 68), and she comes to recognize a grand process of collusion between nuclear scientists, Hollywood directors who make films about star warriors, and politicians, all joined in a "maelstrom of death" (*S,* 72). Not coincidentally, before going to sleep she reads Joseph Conrad's *Heart of Darkness,* a detail that establishes an obvious parallel between the savagery at the heart of colonial civilization, in its exploitation and mistreatment of native populations, and the enormous destructive potential that has resulted from one of twentieth-century civilization's most sophisticated discoveries, which could be called the colonization of the atom.

The pacifist and environmentalist motivations of Wolf's critique are especially evident in the narrator's question, "At which crossroads did human evolution possibly go so wrong that we linked the satisfaction of our desires with the compulsion to destroy" (*S,* 73). As in "Selbstversuch" and *Kassandra, Störfall* is given feminist overtones insofar as this complex of negative qualities is gendered male. And as in "Selbstversuch," science is associated primarily with men, whom the narrator views as having been hardened as boys and having had the ability to love driven out of them. Men of science, the narrator assumes, would not happily perform a variety of tasks conventionally assigned to women, such as "changing a baby's diaper, cooking, shopping with a child on their arm or in a stroller," doing laundry, cleaning, sewing, and so forth (*S,* 38).

The link between feminism, pacifism, and environmentalism is further strengthened by the association of all these issues with nature as opposed to science and technology: nature is foregrounded to raise the reader's awareness of the extent to which it is in danger of being destroyed by nuclear contamination in the supposed interest of defensive warfare. As the narrator notes, a sentence like "The green is explod-ing" (*S*, 9), normally an innocent way to describe the lush arrival of spring, takes on tainted significance in a book that tracks the effects of a nuclear meltdown. Similarly, the narrator plants seeds, an act symboliz-ing new life, at the same time as she is aware that the soil may be ruined by the death-dealing forces of nuclear fallout.

The contrast between unspoiled nature and the contaminating effects of nuclear power is intimated by the quotations from nature poetry and other works of literature celebrating nature that thread through the text. The incongruous insertion of the first lines of Goethe's famous poem "Mailied" (May Song), "How gloriously nature shines for me!" (*S*, 44), into a narrative that laments the ruination of natural resources by human beings is clearly intended to produce an ironic effect, as is the narrator's attribution to contemporary scientists of the desire of Goethe's Faust to "know what holds nature together in its innermost core" (*S*, 34). Although Wolf upholds conventional gender stereotypes here in gendering nature feminine and the agent who would conquer it and penetrate its secrets masculine, her juxtapositions unmask the tradi-tional literary glorification of nature as no longer appropriate for the nuclear era. As Deborah Janson writes with regard to *Störfall*, "This jux-taposition of what [the narrator] hears and thinks causes the narrator to realize that much of the language and imagery commonly used to describe nature has become obsolete as a result of the nuclear acci-dent."[14] Specifically, the narrative's many allusions to the works of Goethe and Schiller, above all to Schiller's "Ode to Joy," underline the barbarism of the nuclear age by placing it side by side with the wholly incongruous humanistic language and spirit of German neoclassicism.

But *Störfall* is not merely another critique of the evils of nuclear power. What makes the book interesting is the fact that it juxtaposes the negative effects of scientific progress with the positive developments science, in this case medicine, has made. Written with the retrospective knowledge that the operation to remove her brother's brain tumor was successful, the narrative alternates between the narrator's speculations about what he might be experiencing at a given moment, her fears about his condition, and her praise for what the doctors have done for him—all these thoughts of course intermingled with the bits and pieces of information she gleans about the nuclear meltdown and its repercus-sions. Wolf's language is carefully chosen to reflect the fact that the sur-gical removal of a tumor from a human brain and the destructive effects of the nuclear accident are two sides of the same coin—scientific progress. One of the best examples of this two-sidedness is her play on the concept of "radiation." Early in the narrative the narrator mentally sends her brother a "beam of energy" ("Energiestrahl"; *S,* 10), emphasizing that this kind of beam is not dangerous. At another point she takes note of the "radiant sky" ("Der strahlende Himmel"), which then makes her think of radiation treatment ("Bestrahlung"; *S,* 28) as a possible post-operative treatment for her brother. Similarly, Werner Krogmann points out the image of the "glowing core" that is used to refer both to the brother's brain tumor and to the nuclear reactor that has caught on fire.[15] In both cases the metaphor signifies a dangerous entity that must be removed or extinguished.

In all these examples, Wolf calls attention not only to the way in which language has been "contaminated" by technology but to the dual nature of science. She argues not for a retrograde return to a world without technological progress but for careful reflection about what scientists and politicians choose to do with the powers they control. In the last analysis, she suggests in *Störfall,* as so often elsewhere, that feelings of love and support (such as the narrator expresses toward her brother) are the best means for the individual to combat the forces of destruction whose potential has become so enormous in the twentieth century. In one of her imaginary conversations with her brother the narrator muses, "What do people want? . . . They want to experience strong emotions and they want to be loved. Period" (*S,* 38). In response to the narrator's fear that the human brain may have evolved too far, the only hope seems to lie in the human heart.

Chapter Seven

The End of the German Democratic Republic: Controversies

The full extent of the parallels between Christa Wolf and the mythical Cassandra did not become evident until years after Wolf's *Kassandra* was published. Just as Cassandra remained loyal to Troy although its citizens repeatedly ignored her prophecies of its fall, Wolf's criticisms of the East German government, stemming from her commitment to the project of a better socialist state, were in a sense borne out by the demise of the GDR in November 1989. The now-famous "We Are the People" speech she delivered on the Alexanderplatz in East Berlin on 4 November, urging her compatriots to remain in the GDR and work together to improve socialism, implied that the country would otherwise be lost. Like Cassandra, Wolf was predicting the future, unheeded. On 9 November the government opened the Berlin Wall for essentially the same reason it had been constructed 28 years earlier: too many East German citizens were *not* remaining. The Berlin Wall fell on the hopes of Wolf and everyone else who had believed in the future of the GDR, since it soon became apparent that the majority of the East German population wanted nothing more than to become like the West. The state to which Wolf had dedicated so much of her time, energy, and commitment for 40 years was no more.

Wolf's career since the elimination of the Wall has not been smooth. Especially given the popularity of her work in both West and East and the numerous prestigious prizes and honors she has won, it is striking and surprising that she has twice endured major scandals. The first wave of attacks, for the most part leveled by the West German media, was brought on by the publication in 1990 of her narrative *Was bleibt: Erzählung* (*What Remains*), the autobiographical story of a woman writer who is spied on by the State Security Service or Secret Police (Stasi); the second barrage followed the revelations in 1993 concerning Wolf's own brief cooperation with the Stasi more than 30 years earlier. This chapter will offer a survey and assessment of these apparently contradictory episodes, including a discussion of the degree to which Wolf's novel *Sommerstück* (1989; Summer Play), published before but written after *Was bleibt,* can be viewed as an indirect commentary on the controversial narrative. Finally, the chapter will take a look at Wolf's most recent work of fiction, *Medea: Stimmen* (1996; *Medea: A Modern Retelling*), in which the author once again, as in *Kassandra,* returns to the realm of myth in order to make a critical comment on the present.

The Controversy Surrounding *Was bleibt*

The characterization of *Was bleibt* as "probably the last East German book" refers to more than the timing of its appearance.[1] The circumstances of its publication have by now acquired legendary familiarity: written in 1979 but not published until June 1990, the story documents a woman writer's sense of persecution during a period in which she feels that she is being watched by three Stasi agents from a car in front of her apartment. As soon as the book appeared, the West German media— led by the newspapers *Die Zeit,* the *Frankfurter Allgemeine Zeitung,* and *Die Welt*—exploded with attacks on its author. The storm that erupted was all the more turbulent because of Wolf's fame, her enormous success as a writer, her political commitment, the unparalleled respect she commanded among GDR functionaries and officials, and her corresponding affluence and privileges.

Was bleibt was criticized above all for its obviously autobiographical quality, for its sentimentality and banality, for the trivial nature of the oppression suffered by its main character, and for the timing of its publication. I will first briefly recapitulate the main lines of attack on Wolf, then summarize the case of those who defended her, as a point of departure from which to shift the terms of the debate.[2]

In the article that launched the attack on Wolf, *Die Zeit* writer Ulrich Greiner lambastes the obvious lack of fiction in *Was bleibt;* in his view the absence of distance between the first-person narrator and the author, along with the careful recording of the trivial events of a day in her life, renders the text comparable to a piece of documentary literature. At the same time he laments Wolf's tendency to avoid concreteness about important details of time, place, and identity (for example, the reader is never told the profession of either the woman narrator or the men observing her) and sees the story's vagueness as going hand in hand with a mood of "gentle renunciation" and "melancholy sentimentality" that appears to drive him to distraction (reprinted in *EG*, 66–70). Frank Schirrmacher, literary editor of the *Frankfurter Allgemeine Zeitung*, goes even further in this direction, condemning Wolf's new book as "so sentimental and unbelievable that it borders on kitsch" (*EG*, 87).

Much more serious than these criticisms on aesthetic grounds, however, were the politically motivated attacks on Wolf. According to Greiner, compared with the genuine suffering endured by so many at the hands of the Stasi—terrorization, torture, and other life-threatening practices—the spying experienced by the narrator of *Was bleibt* is a "trifle" (EG, 67; indeed, another journalist notes that she never definitively establishes whether the car parked outside is watching her or one of her neighbors).[3] To Greiner the publication of the book thus represents the height of insensitivity toward those whose lives were ruined by the communist state. Similarly *Die Welt*'s Jürgen Serke, ironically echoing Wolf's title, writes, "What remains is shame."[4]

But the most frequently made and far-reaching political attack centered on the timing of the book's publication, which Greiner characterizes as "embarrassing" (*EG*, 67). Publication of the book before the demise of the GDR would have caused Wolf considerable difficulties; she would most likely have had to emigrate. To release it when it was no longer dangerous shows not only cowardice but also opportunism, her critics argued.

Wolf's attackers further pointed out that, in contrast to many who had opposed the regime, she had never left it; indeed, she had not even openly criticized institutions such as the terrorization tactics and spy system of the Stasi, the walling-up of the country, or the order to shoot to kill anyone attempting to escape it. They likewise resuscitated the story, disseminated by *FAZ* critic Marcel Reich-Ranicki in 1987, that although she initially signed the 1976 petition protesting the forced expatriation of radical folksinger Wolf Biermann, she soon withdrew her signature, a rumor that Wolf has denied.

And yet the fact remains that Wolf felt she was being watched by the Stasi, documented her sense of persecution and rage in a narrative, but only published that narrative more than ten years later, when the implicated government no longer existed. This set of circumstances provides the key to the question of why this brief work of a scant hundred pages unleashed such a furor. The answer is that it alone did not, since the issue at stake is the relationship of the East German intelligentsia to power. Behind the controversy lies the uncomfortable suspicion that the intellectuals of the GDR were complicit in the oppression exerted by its regime. Hence Greiner's notorious and often quoted response to rejoinders made to attacks on Wolf: "The dead souls of real existing socialism can go to hell."[5]

On the other side of the controversy, voices rose up at both ends of the geographical spectrum on behalf of Wolf. In the West, Günter Grass, Walter Jens, and other liberal intellectuals leapt to her defense at conferences, podium discussions, and in print. In the former GDR, Günter de Bruyn argued that the criticism of Christa Wolf was illogical, unjust, and the result of her success, a reason that often provokes people to overturn monuments; the noted East German dramatist Heiner Müller termed the campaign against her a "Stalinism of the West" (quoted by Greiner, *EG,* 215). Wolf Biermann, responding to the antagonists' question of why Wolf is only now publishing *Was bleibt,* asks why they choose only now to attack her, when it likewise costs nothing (*EG,* 140; all passages cited from this collection first appeared in summer or fall 1990).

Only rarely during the height of the controversy was the narrative examined on its own terms, leaving the debate aside. In one of the most extensive analyses, Herbert Lehnert's focus is linguistic in a double sense; he investigates both Wolf's language in the text and the text's thematization of the difficulties of linguistic communication.[6] The American-based Germanist Josef Modzelewski demonstrates the ways in which the story's language is poetic, compassionate, and occasionally beautiful, but also vague, euphemistic, stylized, lacking in rigor, and sometimes colorless—a duality he attributes to the conflict between Wolf's belief in the power of communism and her awareness of its inadequacies.[7] Similarly, in an issue of *GDR Bulletin* devoted to the controversy, Christiane Zehl Romero takes a close look at the psychology of the text's first-person narrator.[8] Yet most of the other essays in this issue of the *GDR Bulletin,* which are largely supportive of Wolf, focus not on *Was bleibt* per se but on the debate, on the story's place in Wolf's work as a whole, or on her role in the cultural politics of the former GDR.

Emphasizing one side of the conflict in Wolf between her belief in communism and her skepticism toward it, many cite as a defense precisely one of the main reasons she was attacked—the fact that she had never left the GDR. Writing in October 1990, the German-born political scientist Christine Schoefer, now living in the United States, explains this seeming paradox as follows: "The fact that her great disappointment with the Communist regime did not lead her to abandon completely the idea of a more just social order makes Wolf a potentially strong voice in any opposition movement that may arise in a new united Germany, and must be counted among the reasons for the current campaign against her."[9] To this line of thinking Anna Kuhn adds the factor of gender: "It hardly seems coincidental that the all-male coterie that attacked Wolf directed its invective against a writer whose feminist analyses have fundamentally challenged male dominance and hegemonic culture."[10]

The use of the campaign against Wolf as a means to discredit her beliefs and to eradicate the presence of East Germany from the new united Germany was bound up with what many saw as the anticommunist motivation of the attacks. The West German Pen Club went so far as to brand the campaign against Wolf a "species of postmodern McCarthyism."[11] (In this connection one cannot help noting that it is quite an accomplishment for any phenomenon to be labeled both "Stalinism" and "McCarthyism"!)

Wolf's defenders were not limited to the intelligentsia; people wrote to newspapers from all over Germany on her behalf. The letter of a man from Munich to *Die Zeit,* suggesting that *Was bleibt* is not too late but rather arrives at precisely the time when East Germans must concern themselves with their postwar history in order to learn from it with their newfound self-confidence, is representative.[12]

As for Wolf's own reaction, her rationalization that she did not want to publish something in the West that could not be published in the East is rather unconvincing, given the fact that she had previously published two versions of her narrative *Kassandra.* She remarked early in the controversy that with the exception of two instances on the part of party newspaper *Neues Deutschland,* she had never been subjected to a comparable persecution campaign; later she noted that *Was bleibt* seemed to be incomprehensible in the West, whereas it was understood without effort in the East.[13] Yet she did not respond systematically to the attacks made on her, and her silence was telling, indeed resounding.

Sommerstück

I would like to suggest that in a sense Wolf had already responded to the issues at stake in the controversy around *Was bleibt,* in the novel published just before it, *Sommerstück* (Summer Play). I therefore think it would be helpful to deflect attention away from the debate surrounding *Was bleibt* and shed indirect light on it by looking instead at this parallel work. Less a novel than a series of vignettes and impressions, *Sommerstück* recalls selected events in the daily lives of a group of friends during a summer spent years before in a village in Mecklenburg. The impressions are recounted by a third-person narrator who both takes part in the activities of the summer described and assumes an omniscient stance, having access to the thoughts of the other participants.

Upon publication of *Sommerstück,* Fritz Raddatz heralded it as an "idyllic elegy" and "a small great masterpiece" that should at last garner for Wolf the Nobel Prize she had so long deserved.[14] Other West German critics were not nearly so sanguine, claiming that the book merited not the Nobel Prize but the booby prize. *Sommerstück* was attacked for some of the same reasons for which *Was bleibt* was to be lambasted two years later: it was overly concerned with trivial details, sentimental to the point of kitsch, and limited in its clearly autobiographical perspective. Regarding the last of these features, in addition to the close correspondence between the novel's characters and Wolf's own family and friends, we have the "chronicle" *Allerlei-Rauh* as a kind of key. Published in 1988 by the poet Sarah Kirsch, this narrative recalls many of the same events from the same summer, when Kirsch was a guest in the village for a time, but in contrast to Wolf's novel Kirsch's book uses the real names of the people portrayed (Christa, Gerhard, and so forth).

For the purpose of illuminating the controversy around *Was bleibt,* it is important to take note of the process of composition and publication of *Sommerstück:* the events described occurred in the summer of 1975, the novel was written in 1982 and 1983, it was revised in 1987 and was published in 1988. In other words, its genesis was very similar to that of *Was bleibt,* which was written in 1979, revised in 1989, and published in 1990. My point is not that *Was bleibt* was attacked on the basis of its delayed publication whereas *Sommerstück* was not; this disparity, of course, stems from the far more serious comment on the GDR being made by *Was bleibt.* Rather, chronology is significant here because it allows us to see that, although *Was bleibt* appeared after *Sommerstück,* the events that inspired *Was bleibt,* as well as Wolf's first attempts to come to terms with them in writing, preceded the writing of *Sommerstück.* While she may not have published the notorious *Was bleibt* before the regime it implicated had ceased to exist, she did write and publish *Sommerstück,* which if read closely emerges as a questioning of the privileges and self-indulgences of the East German intelligentsia and even hints at its demise. *Sommerstück* is thus the indirect comment on the guilt Wolf felt for not publishing *Was bleibt* at the time she wrote it. The response for which both her attackers and her defenders were waiting from June 1990 on had already been written.

It is not necessary to rely on the autobiographical foundation of *Sommerstück* to recognize the thrust of its commentary, since it is clear from the text alone that its action revolves around a group of intellectuals: the characters called Ellen, Steffi, and Jan are writers, Clemens a painter, Bella a poet, etc. Indeed, the fact that (as we know from outside sources) Ellen is based on Wolf herself, Jan on her husband Gerhard Wolf, Steffi on Maxie Wander, and Bella on Sarah Kirsch even serves to undermine the wider validity of the statements the book is making. These statements are given direction and tone by a web of intertextual references to the work of an author one would not immediately associate with a postwar German writer in the East or West: Anton Chekhov. Reading the novel through the lens of its references to the Russian playwright, both direct and indirect, illuminates the nature of its cultural criticism and thus highlights Wolf's implicit response to the questions that were to arise in the controversy around *Was bleibt*.

The most obvious of these references to Chekhov is the one that gives the novel its title. The group of friends decide to put on a play that they describe as "a loose adaptation of Chekhov," and the list of characters also reveals the work to be not a specific play by him but rather "Chekhovian": a lonely young girl besieged in a rural idyll by her lover, a university professor from the city, a mysterious beauty who dominates everyone around her, a naive girl, a pushy photographer from the city, a grandmother, and so on.[15] Yet significantly Irene, the character who hits on the idea of the play, suggests that "we should all play ourselves" (*SS*, 144), and Ellen's daughter Jenny, the director, exclaims, "Nothing at all will be imagined here. . . . We are, after all, in the middle of a play. Here everything is pure reality" (*SS*, 156). The line between the action of the novel and the action of the Chekhovian play embedded within it is even more blurred by the fact that in the end the friends decide to title the latter "Summer Play." Hermeneutically, then, the entire novel is put on a par with a Chekhovian drama whose parts are acted out by Wolf's characters. By analogy, as in Chekhov, not simply a small group of individuals but an entire social group, even an entire way of life, becomes the object of Wolf's critical commentary.

Much in the text elaborates on this analogy. A nostalgic tone similar to that in which so many of Chekhov's figures speak is created by the temporal distance the narrator perceives between the summer about which she is writing and the time at which she is writing, when so much from that unique period has been lost: "Back then—that's how we talk today—we really lived" (*SS,* 7). Numerous statements call attention to this distance, for instance pointing to the fact that certain features present in the landscape that summer may have since disappeared.

Yet if Raddatz's designation of Wolf's novel as an elegy is apt, his designation of it as idyllic, along with other critics' emphasis on its sentimentality, overlooks the considerable suffering that infiltrates the memorable summer recounted. The main source of the suffering experienced by Wolf's characters is indicated by the first title they suggest for the play they act out, "Love as Imprisonment." The prevalence of frustrated love is the most obvious and extensive parallel to the plays of Chekhov, in particular *The Sea Gull* (1896), which the friends in Wolf's novel single out as "heart-rending" in its "fatal passions" (*SS,* 148). In *The Sea Gull,* in which virtually all the characters either suffer from unrequited love or are loved by someone they do not love or both, the physician Dr. Dorn provides an accurate diagnosis of the situation: (Speaking to Masha, the daughter of his married lover) "How nervous you all are! How nervous! And so much love!"[16]

The same observation could be made with reference to the characters in Wolf's novel. The narrator pays a good deal of attention to the amorous frictions between all the couples: the tensions between Luisa and Antonis, who pines for his native Greece, manifest themselves in her refusal to speak to him for days on end and in the condition that the narrator, entering Luisa's mind, describes as "deathly sad" (*SS,* 35); Irene tortures herself with jealousy over a suspected involvement between her husband Clemens and Luisa, then enters into a flirtation with Jenny's boyfriend Anton (the use of the two names Anton and Antonis in the novel suggests that Wolf might in this way be playfully underlining its affinity to Chekhov's work); attention is even called to tensions between Ellen and Jan—to the point of her thinking in one instance that she hates him and of his being moved to scream at her for irritating him. But the novel's most telling instances of the self-indulgent unproductivity of amorous suffering is perhaps the case of Bella, who is so wounded by the lover who abandoned her that she can no longer write poetry but only accusing letters to him.

That Bella then tears up the letters to her lover instead of sending them is symptomatic of another Chekhovian syndrome in *Sommerstück,* the gap between intention and action. Ellen's speculation that inner pressure increases when the outer world blocks every possibility for action is typical of the attempts of Wolf's characters to rationalize their frequent inability to translate wish into activity. Frauke Meyer-Gosau's characterization of this repeated failure to follow through is apt: "Self-doubts that do not lead to change. Questions that are touched on but not pursued."[17] By comparison, Chekhov's drama could well be called a drama in the subjunctive, filled as it is with people talking about what they might have been. The two wayward shots that the title character of *Uncle Vanya* (1897) fires at Professor Serebryakov, whom he envies for his professional success and his beautiful young wife, can be seen as a symbol of the abortive nature of Vanya's life—a life that has missed its target. Arkadina's brother Sorin in *The Sea Gull* is quintessentially Chekhovian in his lament that he wanted to marry and never did, wanted to become a writer and did not, wanted to live in town and is ending his life in the country.

Nearly a hundred years later, the nostalgic fantasy of Ellen's husband Jan in *Sommerstück,* who wonders what his life would have been like if he had become a forest warden, living with nature rather than with books, with a different wife and children, is strikingly reminiscent of Sorin's. Similarly, Ellen suffers over the realization "that I, like everyone, have become accustomed to never doing exactly what I want to do. Never saying exactly what I want to say. So that without noticing it, I probably no longer think what I want to think" (*SS,* 99). Her sense of impotence is illuminated by the example of Chekhov's *The Three Sisters* (1900), which begins with Olga's voicing of the sisters' wish to return to Moscow, a wish reiterated throughout the play and yet one that will clearly remain unfulfilled. The sisters' other plans also fail: having married young, Masha gradually realizes that her husband is a buffoon; Olga insists that she will not become a headmistress, yet in the end she becomes one; and after Irina finally makes up her mind to marry Baron Tuzenbach, he is killed in a duel. Olga's weary observation sums up their condition: "Nothing ever happens the way we want it to" (*PS,* 279).

The Chekhov play most illustrative of the gap between intention and action is perhaps *The Cherry Orchard* (1903), the very title of which is an emblem of unrealized intentions. Nearly every character in the play makes at least one lyrical reference to the cherry orchard, underlining its idyllic qualities as a symbol of spring, youth, and happiness, although it clearly represents an older way of life whose time has passed. In this connection it is difficult to overlook the impression made on Ellen in *Sommerstück* by the cherry tree on her land, which we have encountered in other works by Wolf such as the Frankfurt lectures and *Störfall*. In *Sommerstück,* the cherry tree is Ellen's foremost visual memory of that unforgettable summer.

As in Chekhov's plays, which typically include a heavily autobiographical figure among the characters whom the author both satirizes and sympathizes with (often a medical doctor, like Chekhov himself), the autobiographical figures in Wolf's novel reflect both her identification with and her critical distance from the milieu on which she is commenting. Intimating her own troubled feelings about her failure to make public the Stasi incident at the foundation of *Was bleibt,* she focuses not on the action but on the lack of action of the characters in *Sommerstück,* not on their political views but on the apolitical nature of their life in the country—their feelings, their amorous adventures, their social gatherings. By revealing—through the analogy of Chekhov—the dark underside of their apparent rural idyll, she strives to come to terms both with her own personal guilt and with that of the East German intelligentsia at large for the injustices perpetrated by their regime.

This dark underside is further manifested in the novel's insights about the vexed nature of human communication, another dominant theme of Chekhov's plays. His peculiar dialogue is often no genuine dialogue at all but rather a talking past, a language of misunderstanding and misdirection. Two highly Chekhovian moments in *Sommerstück* include the story of a neighbor of Ellen's who has recently been united with her sister following a life apart, yet who is unable to communicate with her because she speaks only German and the sister only Polish, and the incident in which a local mailman freezes to death after his former married lover refuses to let him in from where he is lying in the snow because she thinks he is drunk and wants to take up with her again, when in fact he has broken his leg.

Paralleling the characters' difficulties communicating and frustrations over their amorous misadventures and unrealized intentions is a mood of ennui and malaise that further links *Sommerstück* to Chekhov's plays. The wayward cuckoo whose interminable calls are noted by nearly every character in the novel seems to symbolize the repetitious sameness of their lives in the country, punctuated by little activity other than regularly spaced meals. Reminiscent of many of Chekhov's somnambulant figures, Wolf's Clemens intends to defer until his old age the life he knows he is not living now. Ellen often feels herself falling into an "abyss of sorrow" (*SS,* 83), and near the end of the novel she asks the dying Steffi, "Have you ever thought about all the people for whom there is no hope? Once you've learned how to recognize them, you see them everywhere" (*SS,* 212). The narrator remarks of Luisa, "She knew with certainty that it was not her purpose in life to be happy" (*SS,*

116)—a statement recalling the philosophical observation of Lieutenant Colonel Vershinin in *The Three Sisters* that "Happiness is something we never have, but only long for" (*PS*, 240). Similarly, like Chekhov's plays, Wolf's novel abounds in references to transience, aging, and death.

And yet what should not be forgotten is that both Chekhov and Wolf take a critical stance toward the social habits they document. Just as Chekhov became disillusioned with the mid-nineteenth-century reformers who thought the world could be changed overnight, just as he came to believe that change depends on the individual, Wolf suggests that the privileged, self-involved way of life led by the characters in *Sommerstück* is in need of alteration. Early in the novel Ellen declares to Jan, "I think we ought to live differently. Completely differently" (*SS*, 24). An atmosphere of foreboding overshadows the entire book, created early on with Luisa's warning to Ellen that she should not waste a single moment, since something terrible is about to happen. The increasing danger of fires caused by a summer-long drought deepens this sense of doom, and when the "terrible thing" actually does occur and Ellen's and Jan's field catches fire, her feeling of guilt is so great that she envisions their house burning down (as it—and the Wolfs'—later does) and views this disaster as the punishment for their relative affluence: "The house was burning, the house was burning. Things have gone too well for us" (*SS*, 197).

In *Sommerstück* it is thus not the cherry orchard but the house itself that plays a role comparable to that of Chekhov's cherry orchard: the embodiment of the way of life of a particular social structure or group, in Chekhov's case the feudal order, in Wolf's the GDR intelligentsia. Both met their ends through revolution. Not insignificantly, Wolf quotes the Russian playwright in the midst of the German Revolution. At a political discussion following a reading given in October 1989, she brings up the metaphor Chekhov had once formulated: "He had to 'press the slave out of himself drop by drop.' "[18] By the time Wolf had pressed the slave out of herself—by the time she published *Sommerstück* —the house emblematic of her privileges as a successful writer in the GDR had in fact burned down. By the time she published *Was bleibt* two years later, much more had disappeared: the entire East German state.

The Stasi Affair

Barely two years after the debate over *Was bleibt* had begun to die down, Wolf became embroiled in controversy again. With the opening of the Wall and the dismantling of the East German government came also the

unveiling of the dark secret apparatus at its core: the massive bureaucracy of the Stasi, whose agents had amassed more than 100 miles of
files, was cracked open and exposed to the public. As mentioned in
chapter 3, it is now estimated that one in 50 citizens of the GDR were
connected to the Stasi, either as full-time employees or as collaborators.
The metaphorical rendering of the Stasi as an octopus, its poisonous ten-
tacles reaching into virtually every corner of East German life, appeared
in the West German media as early as March 1990 and persisted in the
popular and intellectual imagination.[19] Under the leadership of Joachim
Gauck, a West German commission was established to investigate
cases of suspected collaboration with the Stasi. The Gauck Commission
established a policy whereby GDR citizens could read their so-called
"victim files" but not their "IM files" (*informeller Mitarbeiter,* or "informal
collaborator/informant"), that is, they could read the Stasi's accounts of
its spying and surveillance activities concerning themselves but not the
Stasi's version of information that they had divulged to the Secret Police
about others.

   Availing herself of the Gauck policy, in the spring of 1992 Wolf read
the victim files on herself (and her husband), which consist of some 42
volumes describing the Stasi's surveillance of her from 1968 to 1980;
the files for the following nine years had been largely destroyed. This
experience alone was troubling enough, but far more disturbing was
Wolf's discovery in reading her victim file that she also had a collaborator file, documenting information she had supplied the Stasi in conversations between 1959 and 1962. At the time she was allowed only to
glance at that file, however, and the following fall she took up a year-
long position as visiting scholar at the Getty Institute in Santa Monica,
California.

   But this scholar's paradise was soon to be invaded. In January 1993 it
became public that Christa Wolf (and Heiner Müller) possessed an *IM*
file. The ensuing West German media attack on Wolf was if anything
more vehement than the one that followed the publication of *Was bleibt;*
indeed, some of the same voices are heard, such as those of Schirrmacher
and Raddatz.[20] The language now used to lambaste Wolf is worthy of
careful attention. Portraying her variously as the fallen state writer, as
Cassandra, and as Margarete (the code name assigned to Wolf as Stasi
informant, which she claimed to have forgotten), these articles often use
the same mythologizing language to decry her that had earlier been
used to celebrate her, vividly demonstrating Roland Barthes' thesis that

myths often function as empty signifiers that can be filled with whatever content is most effective for a given rhetorical purpose.[21]

During the winter of 1993 West German journalists made the long trip to California in pursuit of the author; intellectuals debated the issues on German television. How was it possible that the writer whose most recent book complained of her surveillance by the Secret Police had herself collaborated with them? And to what extent had East German intellectuals been complicit in the regime they had supposedly criticized? During the height of the controversy, Wolf was largely silent. There was no denying the facts: the file on her "collaboration" was publicized, there for all to see. But the remarks she made eight months later during a public discussion of the Stasi affair held in Berlin offer a candid insight into her feelings at the time the news hit the press: "I try to talk as openly as possible about the different stages, about the initial shock, the horror at myself, my despair because it seemed impossible—in the midst of the universal Stasi-hysteria—that the public would draw distinctions, about the danger of identifying with the public image of myself."[22] For Wolf, the Stasi affair was nothing short of traumatic.

In explanation of Wolf's actions, it should be noted that her willingness to talk to Stasi agents at all during the late 1950s and early 1960s is bound up with her belief in Marxism and her loyalty at the time to the party, feelings that were all the stronger because they were based on her opposition to fascism, which she had experienced first-hand. On a more practical level, some of the conversations recounted in Wolf's *IM* file were held in her home in the presence of her husband, so that she did not attach confidential status to them; moreover, what she told the Secret Police did not differ from what she published in the press as a literary critic.[23]

It is probably at least in part for these reasons that Wolf made nothing more of her conversations with Stasi agents, forgot that she had had a code name, forgot that she had written a report for the secret police— or repressed these activities—and was shocked to learn that a collaborator file had been established on her. In all likelihood the Stasi gave up on her as an informal collaborator in 1962 because it was not getting the kind of information it wanted. By 1965, Wolf was openly criticizing the regime at the Eleventh Plenum of the Central Committee of the Socialist Unity Party because of its crackdown on the arts, and by 1968 the Stasi had opened its victim file on her. The duration and magnitude of that file, in contrast to the slim file documenting her activity as a supposed informant, literally speak volumes.

Medea: Stimmen

Wolf has often acknowledged that she has been helped through times of crisis and depression by writing, that writing is a kind of therapy for her. Out of her depression over the increasingly stringent censorship of the arts in the mid-1960s grew her work on *Nachdenken über Christa T.;* and the severe crisis she underwent after the expulsion of Wolf Biermann in 1976 and its repercussions for her led to the writing of *Kein Ort. Nirgends.* Similarly, the mental anguish Wolf has endured because of the controversies over *Was bleibt* and the revelations about her Stasi file, as well as her deep disappointment over the disappearance of the GDR and its assimilation into the Federal Republic, have led to the publication of two major recent works: *Auf dem Weg nach Tabou: Texte 1990–1994* (1994; *Parting from Phantoms: Selected Writings, 1990–1994*), and *Medea: Stimmen* (1996; *Medea: A Modern Retelling*). The first of these works contains essays demonstrating the progression in Wolf's thinking from her Alexanderplatz speech of 4 November 1989, in which she speaks compellingly in favor of East German autonomy, to a stance urging both East and West Germany in 1994 to bid farewell to the "phantom" that each has been to the other for so long, so that Germans from all over can sit down at one table and break bread together (*AW,* 337–39).

Wolf's *Medea* also indirectly treats the relationship between the two former German states that now make up one, but it deals with much else besides. The image of Medea as sorceress who commits irrational infanticide was long shaped by Euripides' tragedy (431 B.C.), entitled after its heroine: in the final scene Medea appears before Jason in a chariot drawn by dragons, beside her the bodies of their two sons, whom she has killed in revenge for Jason's opportunistic marriage to the daughter of the king of Corinth. Medea's bitterness is magnified by the fact that it was only with the aid of her magic that Jason had managed to win the Golden Fleece in Colchis and bring it—and her—back to Corinth. The murder of the princess is particularly gruesome: as a wedding gift Medea sends her a poisoned dress that bursts into flames and eats her alive when she puts it on; when her horrified father throws himself down next to her body, he too is devoured by the fiery poison.

Euripides' Medea, called a tiger and a Scylla and described as mad with love, raving, raging, frightening, and acting out of sexual jealousy, represents the quintessential externalization of male fears about the power of female sexuality in fifth-century B.C. Athens. For more than two millennia Medea continued to be portrayed in art and literature as a female monster, because the murder of her children, rendering her the archetypal anti-mother, violated the most sacred principle of female behavior. It is worth noting here that when Susan Smith was convicted of drowning her two young sons in 1995, she was labeled a "Medea of today" by the media, a fact that demonstrates the myth's enduring negative connotations. By contrast, recent feminist interpretations view Euripides' Medea as the embodiment of women's dissatisfaction with their relegation to the private sphere and their strict exclusion from public life in Athenian society. Yet these readings uphold the image of Medea as child-murderer.

Wolf's novel belongs to a more specifically German resurgence of interest in the Medea figure, evident in literature, drama, opera, visual art, and film during the past few decades.[24] Like *Kassandra,* Wolf's *Medea* represents a feminist rewriting of a myth that has been colored by its patriarchal transmission for thousands of years. Her new interpretation adds cultural, political, and psychological dimensions to the gender implications of the myth. Past versions of the tale have exploited the ethnic implications of the fact that Medea is from Colchis, located on the eastern shore of the Black Sea, whereas Jason's home is the Greek city-state of Corinth; significantly, when Jason brings Medea back to Corinth after attaining the Golden Fleece in Colchis, she becomes an exile. Wolf injects a note of cultural relativism: although Colchis lies at the end of the world as known at the time and most of its exiles are regarded as barbarian and inferior by the arrogant, well-to-do Corinthians, Colchian society is characterized by significantly greater economic and sexual equality than is Corinth. Women in Colchis have more power than Corinthian women; the Corinthian astronomer Akamas is impressed, for example, by the fact that in Colchis the astronomers are women. The women in Corinth strike Medea as "carefully tamed pets."[25] Whereas the men in Colchis are able to express their emotions freely and can even weep, the Corinthian men cannot.

But the most significant difference between the two regions, as Medea gradually discovers, is that the civilized, wealthy Corinth is founded on an unspeakable crime: King Creon has had his daughter Iphinoe hidden away and then murdered so that she would not succeed him on the throne, claiming that he thought a female leader would be incompetent and represent a throwback to the times when Corinth was ruled by women. Iphinoe was, in other words, a sacrifice for the sake of progress in Corinth. Creon has moreover covered up this crime with a lie, telling his people that Iphinoe had been abducted by a young king who wanted to marry her. As in *Der geteilte Himmel* and *Kassandra,* in *Medea* Wolf employs geographical differences to underline ethical distinctions. The mythic context and the negative portrayal of Greece are reminiscent of *Kassandra,* but the portrayal of cultural differences between lovers evokes associations with *Der geteilte Himmel:* in *Medea,* as in *Der geteilte Himmel* and other East German works depicting lovers separated by the Berlin Wall, the female partner is, not coincidentally, linked to the East and the male to the West, associations that serve to emphasize the relative power of the two nations.

Wolf's nuanced presentation attempts to capture Medea's complex identity not through absolutes but through impressions, through multiple "voices" offering a series of subjective viewpoints that together create a kaleidoscopic collage; we hear monologues not only from Medea but also from Jason, Creon's daughter Glauke, and three invented voices. Nonetheless the reader emerges from this novel with a revised portrait of Medea as a superior individual: superior as a woman, as a healer, as a priestess who unburdens others by encouraging them to speak—to bring their hidden thoughts to a verbal level, in the manner of a therapist—and as the conscience of the public.

Medea serves as public conscience in two ways. As she tells Jason, one of her functions is to give others a "clean conscience" (*M,* 215), but more fatefully for herself, in learning of Creon's murder of his daughter, she becomes aware of the guilt of a public figure. In Wolf's rewriting of the myth, Medea does not commit the crimes traditionally attributed to the Medea figure—the murders of her brother and children—but the Corinthians accuse her of having killed her brother to conceal their actual reason for banishing her: the threat posed by her knowledge of the dark secret at the heart of the city. Here, as always, knowledge is power, and power is something Medea is not allowed to possess. Wolf's transformation of the archetypal anti-mother is even more striking. Before she goes into banishment, Medea takes her children to a temple and begs the priestesses to take care of them. Instead they are stoned to death by a mob of Corinthians.

As in virtually all Wolf's other works, *Medea* has evident autobiographical parallels. There are marked similarities between Colchis and the former GDR and between Corinth and the Federal Republic; in addition to equality between the sexes, Colchis is characterized by an economic equality akin to socialism. Furthermore, the tensions between Corinth and Colchis have much in common with the difficulties between the former West and East Germany since the fall of the Wall. However, because the novel also contains elements that contradict these parallels, there is little point in pursuing them in depth.[26]

Except, perhaps, for one: certain affinities between the title heroine and Christa Wolf. Like her wholly recreated Medea, Wolf has long served as a moral voice, a public conscience. As with Medea, many have sought her advice over the years, either through reading her books or through writing letters to her. Whether readers were struggling with the particular problems posed by life in the GDR or with personal difficulties, she offered counsel and provided models for countless readers, in the form of literature. As Germany continues to evolve under unification, the nature of Wolf's influence will undoubtedly change as well. But it is not likely to cease.

Notes and References

Chapter One

1. Franz Baumer, *Christa Wolf* (Berlin: Colloquium, 1988), 13.
2. Christa Wolf, *Kindheitsmuster: Roman* (Berlin: Aufbau, 1976; reprint, Darmstadt: Luchterhand, 1979), 20. Except where otherwise indicated, all translations are mine. Titles of book-length works by Wolf that have not been translated into English will either be left in German or rendered in English without being italicized or enclosed in quotation marks.
3. Alexander Stephan, *Christa Wolf,* 4th ed. (Munich: Beck, 1991), 13.
4. Günter de Bruyn, "Fragment eines Frauenporträts," in *Liebes-und andere Erklärungen: Schriftsteller über Schriftsteller,* ed. Annie Voigtländer (Berlin: Aufbau, 1972), 410–12.
5. Wolf, "Über Sinn und Unsinn von Naivität," reprinted in Wolf, *Fortgesetzter Versuch: Aufsätze, Gespräche, Essays* (Leipzig: Reclam, 1979).
6. Quoted by Marilyn Sibley Fries, ed., *Responses to Christa Wolf: Critical Essays* (Detroit: Wayne State University Press, 1989), 34.
7. Ibid., 32.

Chapter Two

1. Régine Robin, *Socialist Realism: An Impossible Aesthetic,* trans. Catherine Porter (1986; Stanford: Stanford University Press, 1992), 5–7; hereafter cited in the text.
2. Buehler, *The Death of Socialist Realism in the Novels of Christa Wolf* (Frankfurt/Main: P. Lang, 1984), 33, 34; hereafter cited in the text.
3. *Zur Theorie des sozialistischen Realismus,* ed. Institut für Gesellschaftswissenschaften beim ZK der SED (Berlin: Dietz, 1974), 603.
4. See for example Dmitry Markov, *Socialist Literatures: Problems of Development,* trans. Catherine Judelson (1978; reprint, Moscow: Raduga, 1984), 83–90, 179–84.
5. Christa Wolf, *Moskauer Novelle* (Halle: Mitteldeutscher Verlag, 1961), 10; hereafter cited in the text as *MN*. My translations refer to this edition.
6. Helen Fehervary, "Christa Wolf's Prose: A Landscape of Masks," *Responses to Christa Wolf: Critical Essays,* ed. Marilyn Sibley Fries (Detroit: Wayne State University Press, 1989), 170.
7. Wolf, "Eine Rede," *Lesen und Schreiben: Aufsätze und Betrachtungen* (Berlin: Aufbau, 1972), 23.

8. Katharina von Ankum, *Die Rezeption von Christa Wolf in Ost und West: Von 'Moskauer Novelle' bis "Selbstversuch"* (Amsterdam: Rodopi, 1992), 47–56.

9. See Gail Finney, " 'True Lies' in the Ex-GDR: The Intersection of History and Fiction in the Career of Christa Wolf," *History and Literature: Essays in Honor of Karl S. Guthke,* ed. William C. Donahue and Scott D. Denham (Tübingen: Stauffenburg, 1999). The Stasi affair will be treated more fully in chapter 7.

10. Wolf, "Über Sinn und Unsinn von Naivität," rpt. in Wolf, *Fortgesetzter Versuch: Aufsätze, Gespräche, Essays* (Leipzig: Reclam, 1979), 53.

11. For example, Franz Baumer, *Christa Wolf* (Berlin: Colloquium, 1988), 27.

12. Sonja Hilzinger, *Christa Wolf* (Stuttgart: Metzler, 1986), 12.

13. Anna K. Kuhn, *Christa Wolf's Utopian Vision: From Marxism to Feminism* (Cambridge: Cambridge University Press, 1988), 23.

14. Baumer, *Christa Wolf,* 35.

15. Christiane Zehl Romero, " 'Remembrance of Things Future': On Establishing a Female Tradition," *Responses to Christa Wolf,* ed. Fries, 110.

16. Wolf, *Der geteilte Himmel* (1963; reprint, Munich: Deutscher Taschenbuch Verlag, 1988), 140ff.; hereafter cited in the text as *GH.*

17. Willkie K. Cirker, "The Socialist Education of Rita Seidel: The Dialectics of Humanism and Authoritarianism in Christa Wolf's *Der geteilte Himmel,*" *University of Dayton Review* 13, no. 2 (Winter 1978): 105–11.

18. Wolf, "Dienstag, der 27. September," *Gesammelte Erzählungen* (1981; reprint, Frankfurt/Main: Luchterhand, 1989), 29; hereafter cited in the text as *GE.*

19. Kuhn, *Wolf's Utopian Vision,* 48.

20. Klemens Renoldner, *Utopie und Geschichtsbewusstsein: Versuche zur Poetik Christa Wolfs* (Stuttgart: Heinz, 1981), 78.

21. Alexander Stephan, *Christa Wolf,* 4th ed. (Munich: Beck, 1991), 50. On the debates that took place in the GDR around *Der geteilte Himmel* see also Karin Lau, ed., *Materialien. Christa Wolf: 'Der geteilte Himmel'* (Stuttgart: Klett, 1981), 28–42, and Dieter Sevin, *Christa Wolf: 'Der geteilte Himmel.' 'Nachdenken über Christa T.'. Interpretation* (Munich: Oldenbourg, 1982), 58–61.

22. Theodore Ziolkowski, *Dimensions of the Modern Novel: German Texts and European Contexts* (Princeton: Princeton University Press, 1969), 332–61.

23. Hilzinger, *Christa Wolf,* 18.

Chapter Three

1. Christa Wolf, "Dienstag, der 27. September," *Gesammelte Erzählungen* (1981; reprint, Frankfurt/Main: Luchterhand, 1989), 33; hereafter cited in the text as *GE.*

2. Margit Resch, *Understanding Christa Wolf: Returning Home to a Foreign Land* (Columbia: University of South Carolina Press, 1997), 52–53.

3. On the book's difficult publication history see Wolf's diaries from these years, published in Angela Drescher, ed., *Dokumentation zu Christa Wolf: 'Nachdenken über Christa T.'* (Hamburg: Luchterhand, 1991), 193–213; and Wolfram Mauser and Helmtrud Mauser, *Christa Wolf: 'Nachdenken über Christa T.'* (Munich: Fink, 1987), 116.

4. On the universality of the quest as a formative activity aimed at transcendence see Robert M. Torrance: *The Spiritual Quest: Transcendence in Myth, Religion, and Science* (Berkeley: University of California Press, 1994).

5. Wolf, *Nachdenken über Christa T.* (1968; reprint, Darmstadt: Luchterhand, 1987), 9–10; hereafter cited in the text as *NCT.*

6. Wolf, "Nachdenken über Christa T.," *Wirkungsgeschichte von Christa Wolfs 'Nachdenken über Christa T.,'* ed. Manfred Behn (Königstein: Athenäum, 1978), 26.

7. Christa Thomassen, *Der lange Weg zu uns selbst: Christa Wolfs Roman 'Nachdenken über Christa T.' als Erfahrungs- und Handlungsmuster* (Kronberg: Scriptor, 1977), 25.

8. Drescher, ed., *Dokumentation, 35.*

9. Mauser and Mauser, *Christa Wolf,* 30.

10. Cf. *Till Eulenspiegel: His Adventures,* trans. Paul Oppenheimer (New York: Garland, 1991), xxvi; hereafter cited in the text.

11. Werner Wunderlich, *'Till Eulenspiegel'* (Munich: Fink, 1984), 88.

12. Ingeborg Singer-Lambert, *Till Eulenspiegel: Versuch einer psychoanalytischen Interpretation der Eulenspiegel-Gestalt* (Frankfurt/Main: Herchen, 1987), 142–76.

13. Dieter Meyer and Wilfried Wulff, "Die engagierte Neugestaltung einer mittelalterlichen Volksbuchfigur: 'Dil Ulenspiegel' (1515) als Vorlage für 'Till Eulenspiegel' (1972) von Christa und Gerhard Wolf," *Till Eulenspiegel in Geschichte und Gegenwart,* ed. Thomas Cramer (Bern: P. Lang, 1978), 93–94.

14. Christa Wolf and Gerhard Wolf, *Till Eulenspiegel* (1972; reprint, Hamburg: Luchterhand, 1993), 44–45; hereafter cited in the text as *TE.*

15. Tzvetan Todorov, *The Fantastic: A Structural Approach to a Literary Genre,* trans. Richard Howard (1970; reprint, Ithaca: Cornell University Press, 1975), esp. 24–57.

Chapter Four

1. Sonja Hilzinger, *Christa Wolf* (Stuttgart: Metzler, 1986), 91.

2. Christa Wolf, "Bei Anna Seghers," in *Lesen und Schreiben: Neue Sammlung. Essays, Aufsätze, Reden* (Darmstadt: Luchterhand, 1980), 148.

3. Wolf, "Fortgesetzter Versuch," in *Lesen und Schreiben: Neue Sammlung,* 156, hereafter cited in the text as "FV"; "Das siebte Kreuz," in *Fortgesetzter*

Versuch: Aufsätze, Gespräche, Essays (Leipzig: Reclam, 1979), 190; hereafter cited in the text as "SK."

4. Wolf, "Glauben an Irdisches," in *Lesen und Schreiben: Neue Sammlung,* 138–39; hereafter cited in the text as "GI."

5. Wolf, "Lesen und Schreiben," in *Lesen und Schreiben: Neue Sammlung,* 13, 18; hereafter cited in the text as "LS."

6. Wolf, "Blickwechsel," in *Gesammelte Erzählungen* (1981; reprint, Frankfurt/Main: Luchterhand, 1989), 13; hereafter cited in the text as *GE.*

7. Margit Resch, *Understanding Christa Wolf: Returning Home to a Foreign Land* (Columbia: University of South Carolina Press, 1997), 81.

8. Wolf, *Kindheitsmuster: Roman* (1976; reprint, Darmstadt: Luchterhand, 1979), 147; hereafter cited in the text as *KM.*

9. As Christel Zahlmann points out, the original East German edition of the novel did not include any generic designation; Zahlmann, *Christa Wolfs Reise "ins Tertiär": Eine literaturpsychologische Studie zu 'Kindheitsmuster'* (Würzburg: Königshausen & Neumann, 1986), 5–6.

Chapter Five

1. Patricia Herminghouse, "The Rediscovery of Romanticism: Revisions and Reevaluations," in *Studies in GDR Culture and Society 2,* ed. Margy Gerber (Washington: University Press of America, 1982), 4.

2. Sara Lennox, "Christa Wolf and the Women Romantics," in Gerber, 32.

3. Christa Wolf, "Die zumutbare Wahrheit: Prosa der Ingeborg Bachmann," in *Lesen und Schreiben: Neue Sammlung. Essays, Aufsätze, Reden* (Darmstadt: Luchterhand, 1980), 173; hereafter cited in the text as "ZW."

4. Wolf, "Tagebuchauszüge zu 'Nachdenken über Christa T.,' " in *Dokumentation zu Christa Wolf: 'Nachdenken über Christa T.,'* ed. Angela Drescher (Hamburg: Luchterhand, 1991), 193.

5. See for example Brigitte Peucker, "Dream, Fairy Tale, and the Literary Subtext of 'Unter den Linden,' " in *Responses to Christa Wolf: Critical Essays,* ed. Marilyn Sibley Fries (Detroit: Wayne State University Press, 1989), 303.

6. Wolf, "Unter den Linden," in *Gesammelte Erzählungen* (1981; reprint, Frankfurt/Main: Luchterhand, 1989), 54; hereafter cited as *GE.*

7. Hans-Georg Werner, "Unter den Linden: Three Improbable Stories," in *Responses to Christa Wolf,* ed. Fries, 282–83.

8. Wolf, "Neue Lebensansichten eines Katers," *GE,* 97, 99.

9. Although the conventional spellings are "Bettina" and "Günderode," Wolf alternates between "Bettina" and "Bettine." Regarding the second name, I am following Wolf's orthography, which as she points out conforms to the original family spelling.

10. Wolf, "Der Schatten eines Traumes: Karoline von Günderrode—ein Entwurf," in *Lesen und Schreiben: Neue Sammlung,* 260; hereafter cited in the text as "ST."

11. Wolf, "Nun ja! Das nächste Leben geht aber heute an: Ein Brief über die Bettine," in *Lesen und Schreiben: Neue Sammlung,* 284; hereafter cited as "BB."

12. Wolf, *Kein Ort. Nirgends* (1979; reprint, Darmstadt: Luchterhand, 1981), 5 – 6; hereafter cited in the text as *KN.*

13. Ute Brandes, *Zitat und Montage in der neueren DDR-Prosa* (Frankfurt/Main: P. Lang, 1984), 61–100, quotation is on page 69.

14. Cf. Helga G. Braunbeck, *Autorschaft und Subjektgenese: Christa Wolfs 'Kein Ort. Nirgends'* (Vienna: Passagen Verlag, 1992), who notes that the utterances of the characters should be thought of as emerging not only from their mouths but from the mouth of the narrator as well; "the voice that speaks becomes a double voice" (Braunbeck, 138).

15. Donna K. Reed. "Merging Voices: *Mrs. Dalloway* and *No Place on Earth,*" *Comparative Literature* 47 (Spring 1995): 131.

Chapter Six

1. Christa Wolf, "Fortgesetzter Reisebericht über die Verfolgung einer Spur," in *Voraussetzungen einer Erzählung: Kassandra. Frankfurter Poetik-Vorlesungen* (1983; reprint, Hamburg: Luchterhand, 1990), 75 –76; volume hereafter cited in the text as *VE.*

2. As Anne Herrmann points out, "In Wolf's text it is not the feminine but the masculine that is 'Anders' (that is, posited as Other)"; Herrmann, "The Transsexual as *Anders* in Christa Wolf's 'Self-Experiment,'" *Genders* 3 (1988): 47. But the narrator's addressee constitutes another masculine Other of importance in Wolf's story. See also Herrmann, *The Dialogic and Difference: "An/Other Woman" in Virginia Woolf and Christa Wolf* (New York: Columbia University Press, 1989).

3. For example, Jürgen Nieraad, "Subjektivität als Thema und Methode realistischer Schreibweise: Zur gegenwärtigen DDR-Literaturdiskussion am Beispiel Christa Wolf," *Literatur-Wissenschaftliches Jahrbuch* 19 (1978): 300.

4. Wolf, "Lesen und Schreiben," in *Lesen und Schreiben: Neue Sammlung. Essays, Aufsätze, Reden* (Darmstadt: Luchterhand, 1980), 48.

5. Wolf, "Selbstversuch: Traktat zu einem Protokoll," in *Gesammelte Erzählungen* (1981; reprint, Frankfurt/Main: Luchterhand, 1989), 160, 161; hereafter cited in the text as *GE.*

6. Michel Butor, "L'usage des pronoms personnels dans le roman," *Les temps modernes* 16, no. 178 (1961): 941.

7. Bruce Morrissette, "Narrative 'You' in Contemporary Literature," *Comparative Literature Studies* 2 (1965): 4.

8. Nancy Lukens, "Future Perfect?: Language and Utopia in Christa Wolf's Chernobyl Narrative," unpublished manuscript, 9 –10.

9. Sabine Wilke, *Ausgraben und Erinnern: Zur Funktion von Geschichte, Subjekt und geschlechtlicher Identität in den Texten Christa Wolfs* (Würzburg: Königshausen & Neumann, 1993), 139 – 40.

10. Wolf, *Kassandra: Erzählung* (1983; reprint, Darmstadt: Luchterhand, 1986), 131; herafter cited in the text as *K*.

11. Therese Hörnigk, *Christa Wolf* (Göttingen: Steidl, 1989), 214.

12. Romey Sabalius, "Literatur bleibt!: Der 'Fall' Christa Wolf," in *Schreiben im heutigen Deutschland: Die literarische Szene nach der Wende,* ed. Ursula E. Beitter (New York: P. Lang, 1997), 38.

13. Wolf, *Störfall: Nachrichten eines Tages* (Darmstadt: Luchterhand, 1987), 69; hereafter cited in the text as *S*.

14. Deborah Janson, "In Search of Common Ground: An Ecofeminist Inquiry into Christa Wolf's Work," in *Ecofeminist Literary Criticism: Theory, Interpretation, Pedagogy,* ed. Greta Gaard and Patrick D. Murphy (Urbana: University of Illinois Press, 1998), 182.

15. Werner Krogmann, *Christa Wolf: Konturen* (Frankfurt/Main: P. Lang, 1989), 359.

Chapter Seven

1. Jozef A. Modzelewski, "Christa Wolf und ihr umstrittenes Suchen nach der 'anderen Sprache' im Text *Was bleibt* (1990)" (paper presented at Kentucky Foreign Language Conference, April 1991), 1.

2. For a collection of the most important media pieces in the controversy, see *"Es geht nicht um Christa Wolf": Der Literaturstreit im vereinten Deutschland,* ed. Thomas Anz (Frankfurt/Main: Fischer, 1995); hereafter cited in the text as *EG*. For interpretive essays on the debate, consult *Der deutsch-deutsche Literaturstreit oder "Freunde, es spricht sich schlecht mit gebundener Zunge": Analysen und Materialien,* ed. Karl Deiritz and Hannes Krauss (Hamburg: Luchterhand, 1991).

3. Eric Hansen, "The Writer Whom the Wall No Longer Protects," *The European,* 3–5 Aug. 1990, 3.

4. Serke, "Was bleibt, das ist die Scham," *Die Welt,* 23 June 1990, 17.

5. Greiner, "Der Potsdamer Abgrund," *Die Zeit,* 22 June 1990, 59.

6. Lehnert, "Fiktionalität und autobiographische Motive: Zu Christa Wolfs Erzählung 'Was bleibt,' " *Weimarer Beiträge* 37, no. 3 (1991): 423–44.

7. Modzelewski, "Christa Wolf."

8. Zehl Romero, "Was bleibt," *GDR Bulletin* 17 (Spring 1991): 1–3.

9. Schoefer, "The Attack on Christa Wolf," *The Nation,* 22 Oct. 1990, 448–49.

10. Kuhn, "Rewriting GDR History: The Christa Wolf Controversy," *GDR Bulletin* 17 (Spring 1991): 10.

11. Quoted in Greiner, "Dumm und dämlich," *Die Zeit,* 13 July 1990, 43.

12. Letter from Uwe Jüttner, " 'Schwierigkeiten, mit der Wahrheit fertig zu werden,' " *Leserbriefe, Die Zeit,* 29 June 1990, 22.

13. Quoted by Arno Widmann, "Bitte um Aufklärung," *taz*, 14 June 1990, 17; second statement quoted in " 'Es ist ein anderes Leben,' " *Der Spiegel*, 24 Sept. 1990, 40.

14. Raddatz, "Ein Rückzug auf sich selbst," *Die Zeit*, 24 March 1989, 2.

15. Christa Wolf, *Sommerstück* (Frankfurt/Main: Luchterhand, 1989), 144; hereafter cited in the text as *SS*.

16. Anton Chekhov, *The Sea Gull*, in *Plays and Stories*, trans. Ann Dunnigan (New York: International Collectors Library, 1960), 98; hereafter cited in the text as *PS*.

17. Meyer-Gosau, "Am Ende angekommen: Zu Christa Wolfs Erzählungen *Störfall, Sommerstück* und *Was bleibt*," *Literatur für Leser* 2 (1990): 89.

18. Wolf, " 'Das haben wir nicht gelernt,' " *Wochenpost*, 27 Oct. 1989, 3.

19. David Bathrick, *The Powers of Speech: The Politics of Culture in the GDR* (Lincoln: University of Nebraska Press, 1995), 220.

20. For a collection of the media responses to this revelation as well as helpful background material, see Hermann Vinke, ed., *Akteneinsicht Christa Wolf: Zerrspiegel und Dialog. Eine Dokumentation* (Hamburg: Luchterhand, 1993).

21. See Gail Finney, " 'True Lies' in the Ex-GDR: The Intersection of History and Fiction in the Career of Christa Wolf," in *History and Literature: Essays in Honor of Karl S. Guthke*, ed. William C. Donahue and Scott D. Denham (Tübingen: Stauffenburg, 1999).

22. Wolf, "Berlin, Montag, der 27. September 1993," in *Auf dem Weg nach Tabou: Texte 1990–1994* (Cologne: Kiepenheuer & Witsch, 1994), 291; hereafter cited in the text as *AW*.

23. Bathrick, *Powers of Speech*, 224.

24. See Simone Novak, "The Return of the Medea: Bridging Dichotomies in Contemporary German Culture" (Ph.D. diss., University of California, Davis, 1998), which examines the recent resurgence of interest in the Medea figure with the aid of psychoanalysis.

25. Wolf, *Medea: Stimmen*. (Munich: Luchterhand, 1996), 18; hereafter cited in the text as *M*.

26. Cf. Herbert Lehnert, "Stimmen von Macht und Freiheit: Christa Wolf, *Medea*," in *Literatur und Geschichte: Festschrift für Wulf Koepke zum 70. Geburtstag*, ed. Karl Menges (Amsterdam: Rodopi, 1998), 301–02. For an analysis juxtaposing Wolf's *Medea* with Botho Strauß's *Ithaka* as evidence of the close relationship between national and mythic discourses in the postmodern era, see Inge Stephan, *Musen und Medusen: Mythos und Geschlecht in der Literatur des 20. Jahrhunderts* (Cologne: Böhlau Verlag, 1997), 233–52.

Selected Bibliography

PRIMARY SOURCES

Original Works

FICTION

Moskauer Novelle. Halle: Mitteldeutscher Verlag, 1961.
Der geteilte Himmel: Erzählung. Halle: Mitteldeutscher Verlag, 1963.
Nachdenken über Christa T. Halle: Mitteldeutscher Verlag, 1968.
Till Eulenspiegel: Erzählung für den Film (with Gerhard Wolf). Berlin: Aufbau, 1972.
Unter den Linden: Drei unwahrscheinliche Geschichten. Berlin: Aufbau, 1974.
Kindheitsmuster: Roman. Berlin: Aufbau, 1976.
Kein Ort. Nirgends. Berlin: Aufbau, 1979.
Gesammelte Erzählungen. Darmstadt: Luchterhand, 1980.
Kassandra: Erzählung. Darmstadt: Luchterhand, 1983.
Störfall: Nachrichten eines Tages. Berlin: Aufbau, 1987.
Sommerstück. Berlin: Aufbau, 1989.
Was bleibt: Erzählung. Berlin: Aufbau, 1990.
Medea: Stimmen. Roman. Munich: Luchterhand, 1996.

ESSAYS, SPEECHES, CONVERSATIONS, LETTERS

Lesen und Schreiben: Aufsätze und Prosastücke. Darmstadt: Luchterhand, 1972.
Fortgesetzter Versuch: Aufsätze, Gespräche, Essays. Leipzig: Reclam, 1979.
Lesen und Schreiben: Neue Sammlung. Essays, Aufsätze, Reden. Darmstadt: Luchterhand, 1980.
Voraussetzungen einer Erzählung: Kassandra. Frankfurter Poetik-Vorlesungen. Darmstadt: Luchterhand, 1983.
"Ins Ungebundene gehet eine Sehnsucht." Gesprächsraum Romantik: Prosa. Essays (with Gerhard Wolf). Berlin: Aufbau, 1985.
Die Dimension des Autors: Essays und Aufsätze, Reden und Gespräche 1959–1985. Ed. Angela Drescher. Darmstadt: Luchterhand, 1987.
Ansprachen. Darmstadt: Luchterhand, 1988.
Angepaßt oder mündig?: Briefe an Christa Wolf im Herbst 1989. Ed. Petra Gruner. Frankfurt/Main: Luchterhand, 1990.
Im Dialog: Aktuelle Texte. Berlin: Aufbau, 1990.
Reden im Herbst. Berlin: Aufbau, 1990.

Sei gegrüsst und lebe: Eine Freundschaft in Briefen 1964–1973. Brigitte Reimann/ Christa Wolf. Berlin: Aufbau, 1993.

Auf dem Weg nach Tabou: Texte 1990–1994. Cologne: Kiepenheuer & Witsch, 1994.

Monsieur—wir finden uns wieder: Briefe 1968–1984. Franz Fühmann/Christa Wolf. Ed. Angela Drescher. Berlin: Aufbau, 1995.

Unsere Freunde, die Maler: Bilder, Essays, Dokumente (with Gerhard Wolf). Ed. Peter Bothig. Berlin: Janus, 1995.

EDITIONS BY WOLF

In diesen Jahren: Ausgewählte deutsche Prosa. Leipzig: Reclam, 1957.

Proben junger Erzähler. Leipzig: Reclam, 1959.

Wir, unsere Zeit: Prosa und Gedichte aus zehn Jahren (with Gerhard Wolf). 2 vols. Berlin: Aufbau, 1959.

Anna Seghers, *Glauben an Irdisches: Essays aus vier Jahrzehnten.* Leipzig: Reclam, 1969.

Karoline von Günderrode, *Der Schatten eines Traumes: Gedichte, Prosa, Briefe, Zeugnisse von Zeitgenossen.* Berlin: Buchverlag Der Morgen, 1979.

Bettina von Arnim, *Die Günderode.* Leipzig: Insel, 1980.

Anna Seghers, *Ausgewählte Erzählungen.* Darmstadt: Luchterhand, 1983.

English Translations

FICTION

Divided Heaven. Trans. Joan Becker. Berlin: Seven Seas Books, 1965; New York: Adler's Foreign Books, 1976.

The Quest for Christa T. Trans. Christopher Middleton. New York: Farrar, Straus and Giroux, 1970.

Patterns of Childhood (formerly *A Model Childhood*). Trans. Ursule Molinaro and Hedwig Rappolt. New York: Farrar, Straus and Giroux, 1980.

No Place on Earth. Trans. Jan van Heurck. New York: Farrar, Straus and Giroux, 1982.

Cassandra: A Novel and Four Essays. Trans. Jan van Heurck. New York: Farrar, Straus and Giroux, 1984.

Accident: A Day's News. Trans. Heike Schwarzbauer and Rick Takvorian. New York: Farrar, Straus and Giroux, 1989.

What Remains and Other Stories. Trans. Heike Schwarzbauer and Rick Takvorian. New York: Farrar, Straus and Giroux, 1993.

Medea: A Modern Retelling. Trans. John Cullen. New York: Doubleday, 1998.

ESSAYS AND INTERVIEWS

The Reader and the Writer: Essays, Sketches, Memories. Trans. Joan Becker. New York: Signet, 1977.

The Fourth Dimension: Interviews with Christa Wolf. Trans. Hilary Pilkington. London: Verso, 1988.

The Author's Dimension: Selected Essays. Ed. Alexander Stephan. Trans. Jan van Heurck. New York: Farrar, Straus and Giroux, 1993; also published as *The Writer's Dimension,* London: Virago, 1993.

Parting from Phantoms: Selected Writings, 1990–1994. Trans. Jan van Heurck. Chicago: University of Chicago Press, 1997.

SECONDARY SOURCES

Most recent comprehensive bibliography (annotated): de Wild, Henk. *Bibliographie der Sekundärliteratur zu Christa Wolf.* Frankfurt/Main: P. Lang, 1995.

von Ankum, Katharina. *Die Rezeption von Christa Wolf in Ost und West: Von 'Moskauer Novelle' bis 'Selbstversuch.'* Amsterdam: Rodopi, 1992. Detailed evaluative discussions of responses by journalists as well as literary critics to selected works by Wolf.

Anz, Thomas, ed. *"Es geht nicht um Christa Wolf": Der Literaturstreit im vereinten Deutschland.* Frankfurt/Main: Fischer, 1995. Collection of the vociferous media responses to Wolf's publication of *Was bleibt,* given cohesion by Anz's helpful background discussions.

Bathrick, David. *The Powers of Speech: The Politics of Culture in the GDR.* Lincoln: University of Nebraska Press, 1995. Illuminating analysis of the role of the intellectual in the GDR and of the cultural and political context within which Wolf, Heiner Müller, and other artists and thinkers functioned.

Baumer, Franz. *Christa Wolf.* 2nd ed. Berlin: Morgenbuch, 1996. Brief, readable survey of Wolf's life and work.

Braunbeck, Helga G. *Autorschaft und Subjektgenese: Christa Wolfs 'Kein Ort. Nirgends.'* Vienna: Passagen, 1992. Employs poststructuralist theory, above all that of Lacan, Cixous, and Kristeva, to investigate the concepts of authorship, intersubjectivity, and intertextuality in *KN.*

Buehler, George. *The Death of Socialist Realism in the Novels of Christa Wolf.* Frankfurt/Main: P. Lang, 1984. Discussion of the socialist realist doctrine, Wolf's adherence to it in *Moskauer Novelle,* her partial move away from it in *Der geteilte Himmel,* and her break with it in *Nachdenken über Christa T.* and *Kein Ort. Nirgends.*

Deiritz, Karl and Hannes Krauss, eds. *Der deutsch-deutsche Literaturstreit oder "Freunde, es spricht sich schlecht mit gebundener Zunge": Analysen und Materialien.* Hamburg: Luchterhand, 1991. These thoughtful essays focus on the controversy around the publication of *Was bleibt* and in doing so deal also with issues such as the moral responsibility of the intellectual in Germany and the political function of literature. Collection includes reprints of important newspaper articles documenting the controversy.

Drescher, Angela, ed. *Christa Wolf: Ein Arbeitsbuch. Studien-Dokumente-Bibliographie.* Berlin: Aufbau, 1989. Eclectic, somewhat personal collection of essays on Wolf, many of them by other well-known writers and critics, as well as letters and speeches by Wolf.

Firsching, Annette. *Kontinuität und Wandel im Werk von Christa Wolf.* Würzburg: Königshausen & Neumann, 1996. A comprehensive overview that illuminates the stylistic transformations and thematic consistencies in Wolf's major works through *Was bleibt.*

Fries, Marilyn, ed. *Responses to Christa Wolf: Critical Essays.* Detroit: Wayne State University Press, 1989. Collection of insightful essays by noted Wolf specialists on works through *Kassandra,* including pieces on Wolf's relationships to other women writers.

Growe, Ulrike. *Erfinden und Erinnern: Typologische Untersuchungen zu Christa Wolfs Romanen 'Kindheitsmuster,' 'Kein Ort. Nirgends' und 'Kassandra.'* Würzburg: Königshausen & Neumann, 1988. Close comparative analyses of the three texts focusing on the themes of memory, writing, and narration.

Herrmann, Anne. *The Dialogic and Difference: "An/Other Woman" in Virginia Woolf and Christa Wolf.* New York: Columbia University Press, 1989. Employs Bakhtin's concept of the dialogic in studying the construction of the female subject in the woman-centered ideologies of Woolf and Wolf. Discusses nonfictional as well as fictional texts.

Hilzinger, Sonja. *Christa Wolf.* Stuttgart: Metzler, 1986. This survey of Wolf's works through *Kassandra* is distinguished by useful background discussions.

Hörnigck, Therese. *Christa Wolf.* Göttingen: Steidl, 1989. Sensitive analysis of the works though *Störfall* by a friend of Wolf's and fellow East German intellectual. Includes an extensive interview with the author about her life and work, conducted in 1987–1988.

Jankowsky, Karen H. *Unsinn, anderer Sinn, neuer Sinn: Zur Bewegung im Denken von Christa Wolfs 'Kassandra' über den Krieg und die "Heldengesellschaft."* Berlin: Argument, 1989. Close analysis of important concepts in the narrative.

Krogmann, Werner. *Christa Wolf: Konturen.* Frankfurt/Main: P. Lang, 1989. This in-depth study contextualizes major works from *Der geteilte Himmel* through *Störfall* with relation to cultural politics and literary history.

Kuhn, Anna K. *Christa Wolf's Utopian Vision: From Marxism to Feminism.* Cambridge: Cambridge University Press, 1988. The first comprehensive study of Wolf's works in English. Lucid, informed discussions of the prose works from *Moskauer Novelle* to *Störfall.*

Love, Myra N. *Christa Wolf: Literature and the Conscience of History.* New York: P. Lang, 1991. Thoughtful readings of the major works from *Der geteilte*

Himmel through *Kassandra* focusing on Wolf's development as a moralist and as a defender and critic of the heritage of the Enlightenment.

Mauser, Wolfram and Helmtrud. *Christa Wolf: 'Nachdenken über Christa T.'* Munich: Fink, 1987. Designed for use in schools, contains much helpful background material on *NCT* as well as model textual analyses.

Mauser, Wolfram, ed. *Erinnerte Zukunft: 11 Studien zum Werk Christa Wolfs.* Würzburg: Königshausen & Neumann, 1985. Remains one of the best essay collections on Wolf.

Quernheim, Mechthild. *Das moralische Ich: Kritische Studien zur Subjektwerdung in der Erzählprosa Christa Wolfs.* Würzburg: Königshausen & Neumann, 1990. Close analysis of *Nachdenken über Christa T., Kindheitsmuster, Kein Ort. Nirgends,* and *Kassandra* with special attention to the construction of subjectivity and the process of narration.

Renoldner, Klemens. *Utopie und Geschichtsbewußtsein: Versuche zur Poetik Christa Wolfs.* Stuttgart: Heinz, 1981. Examines the earlier works in terms of the illuminating dialectic between historicity and the concept of utopia.

Resch, Margit. *Understanding Christa Wolf: Returning Home to a Foreign Land.* Columbia: University of South Carolina Press, 1997. Highly readable and informative introduction to the life and works from a post-Wall perspective.

Sevin, Dieter. *Christa Wolf: 'Der geteilte Himmel.' 'Nachdenken über Christa T.'. Interpretation.* Munich: Oldenbourg, 1982. Textual interpretations oriented toward high-school and college students.

Stephan, Alexander. *Christa Wolf.* 4th ed. Munich: Beck, 1991. Survey of the life and work by a long-time Wolf scholar.

Vinke, Hermann, ed. *Akteneinsicht Christa Wolf: Zerrspiegel und Dialog. Eine Dokumentation.* Hamburg: Luchterhand, 1993. Newspaper articles, letters, conversations, and other documentation of the controversy following the revelation in January 1993 that, decades earlier, Wolf had briefly served as an informant for the State Security Service (Stasi).

Wallace, Ian, ed. *Christa Wolf in Perspective.* Amsterdam: Rodopi, 1994. A lively collection of essays, some of which take into account the two controversies surrounding the publication of *Was bleibt* and the revelation of Wolf's cooperation with the Stasi.

Wilke, Sabine. *Ausgraben und Erinnern: Zur Funktion von Geschichte, Subjekt und geschlechtlicher Identität in den Texten Christa Wolfs.* Würzburg: Königshausen & Neumann, 1993. Sophisticated analyses of selected works as elucidated variously by new historicism, the writings of Walter Benjamin, feminist theory, and post-structuralist psychoanalytic thought.

Zahlmann, Christel. *Christa Wolfs Reise "ins Tertiär": Eine literaturpsychologische Studie zu 'Kindheitsmuster.'* Würzburg: Königshausen & Neumann, 1986. Uses the tools of psychoanalysis to penetrate the surface of the text.

Index

The Author

Gail Finney is professor of German and comparative literature at the University of California, Davis. She received her A.B. in German from Princeton University and her Ph.D. in comparative literature from the University of California, Berkeley. From 1980 to 1988 she was assistant and then associate professor of German at Harvard University. She has published *The Counterfeit Idyll: The Garden Ideal and Social Reality in Nineteenth-Century Fiction* (1984), *Women in Modern Drama: Freud, Feminism, and European Theater at the Turn of the Century* (1989), and *Look Who's Laughing: Gender and Comedy* (ed.) (1994), as well as articles on numerous aspects of nineteenth- and twentieth-century German and comparative literature. She is currently working on a book entitled *Muted Laughter: Gender and German Comedy.*

The Editor

David O'Connell is professor of French at Georgia State University. He received his Ph.D. in 1966 from Princeton University, where he was a National Woodrow Wilson Fellow, the Bergen Fellow in Romance Languages, and a National Woodrow Wilson Dissertation Fellow. He is the author of *The Teachings of Saint Louis: A Critical Text* (1972), *Les Propos de Saint Louis* (1974), *Louis-Ferdinand Céline* (1976), *The Instructions of Saint Louis: A Critical Text* (1979), and *Michel de Saint Pierre: A Catholic Novelist at the Crossroads* (1990). He has edited more than 60 books in the Twayne World Authors Series.